Growing
VEGETABLES and HERBS

Growing
VEGETABLES

Brombacher Books

and HERBS

Bryce L. Patterson

Richmond, California

Thanks for permission to take or use photographs go to Ferry-Morse
Seed Company, pp. 3, 10, 11, 42, 45, 47, 49, 55, 57-59, 65-68,
70-80, 83-85, 103, 134; and to M. V. Nurseries, Inc., pp. 6, 8,
12, 35, 63. Front cover photo, Ferry-Morse Seed Company; back
cover photo, M.V. Nurseries, Inc.

Mention of a product by trade name in this book is a record of the
author's practice and does not constitute a recommendation for its
use. It must be emphasized that the proper use of any product
requires following the explicit instructions of its manufacturer on the
label or package.

Manufactured in the United States of America.
Library of Congress Catalog Card Number: 74-29673
ISBN: 0-89085-154-9

Contents

Foreword

Our ancestors knew well the value of the land and its capability of producing their nutritional requirements. The reward for their labor was a sense of accomplishment.

Today with the rising cost of commercially grown vegetables and herbs the home gardener can add to that sense of accomplishment the knowledge that he or she has the highest nutritional value for the lowest possible cost with minimal effort.

The author of this book has gathered from many different areas the age old ideas and modern suggestions for ''do it yourself'' vegetable and herb gardening.

The clear, concise text shows you how you can spend rewarding hours with the food growing process in your own backyard, large or ''pocket size,'' in order to utilize all available space with the rotation method of gardening. In this manner not one but several crops may be grown throughout the productive seasons. Simple, time-proven gardening procedures from the planting of the seed to the reaping of the harvest are explained in detail with illustrations, photographs, and charts.

True, the modern methods employed to cultivate and control pests are a definite advantage over original agricultural efforts.

However, the pride of accomplishment, the satisfaction of a job well done and the taste of produce fresh from the garden are unchanged by modern technology.

You, the gardener, will find something very fulfilling in every page of this book. The tables at the back of the book are merely suggestions as to some methods of disease and insect control. However, laws for the use of certain products for specific disease and insect controls may very from place to place. Your local county agricultural agent is ready and willing to provide you with the most up to date recommendations to correct any unusual disease or pest problems.

Mike Vukelich
M.V. Nurseries, Inc.

Introduction

Food prices are soaring. Gasoline costs have doubled in the last year and, according to many commentators, may double again in the near future. It is worth next year's vacation savings just to call a repairman. Everything seems to be going up but the stock market and your salary.

The police will not tolerate city dwellers keeping a cow, and poultry make too much noise, anyway. It is too far to work to take up bicycling and the air conditioner insists it is not going to work properly no matter how many times you kick it.

To add to this year of woes, you keep getting that tingle at the back of your neck wondering if those ecology buffs know something you don't when they claim there is no nutrition in today's store-bought food and that some of the chemicals used in its production are dangerous.

Finally, all the concerns come together. The lush lawn that was your pride last summer, those well-manicured flower beds, and the window boxes of geraniums and petunias are all going to give way to the economic onslaught and start sprouting radishes and tomatoes, squash and lettuce. The mortgage, at least, is going to start paying for itself.

A good backyard corn patch that is just beginning to yield. Note marigolds interplanted to discourage insect pests

In this day of specialized technology, one of the strangest things about the idea of saving money by growing your own food is the fact that it actually can be done. You may not have been reared on a farm, you may not be famous throughout the neighborhood for having a "green thumb," and you may not have all the time in the world—but you can do it. No one knows how many home vegetable plots there are in the country as a whole, but millions of people are growing at least some of their own food, and not all of them are "born farmers."

All it takes to grow a productive garden is some knowledge—not a college degree in horticulture, just a little information on the various aspects of what's involved.

Knowing enough about how things grow to make a successful garden is easy. Man's knowledge of soils, climate, pests, and plant diseases has been accumulating for the many thousands of years since he stopped picking the nuts and berries he found in his hunting travels and settled down to cultivate a plot of ground. What to do about problems and how to take advantage of the positive things

Correct method of watering. Hose is placed on canvas or burlap bag and water trickles down furrows

nature provides for the grower may make a lifelong study for some scientists, but what you and your neighbors need to know to become productive gardeners comes down to a few things that are really very simple.

Disease- and climate-resistant plants have been developed; protective techniques are available; there are fertilizers to enrich practically any soil; and a wide range of methods exists for controlling plant diseases and insect pests.

You do not actually need to know everything about how these things work; what you do need to know is which ones will solve your particular problems. There are a lot of government officials, teachers at agricultural colleges, and garden shop operators quite willing to give you all the help and advice you can use.

Although this book will not get into the realm of commercial farming, everything that has been learned in modern agriculture is available to you and all the home gardeners in your neighborhood.

All it takes to become successful is a little planning of what you want to accomplish, some basic information, and the ability to keep working at something to reach a desired end. The guidance in this book will give you what you need to get started toward keeping your grocery bill within limits and knowing what goes into the food your children are eating.

It may also give you the added benefit of pride in real achievement, a hobby that will endure, and a chance to get some exercise in the open air that will add to the feeling of well-being you get from home-grown, really fresh foodstuffs.

Useful herbs can be easily grown at home. See chapters 5 and 6

1 *Weather*

As a vegetable and herb gardener about the only condition you will meet that is almost beyond your control is the weather. Without proper choice of crops to go with the weather conditions in your area, or knowledge of how to react to weather conditions so that nothing happens to upset your purposes, you will not have much to show for your gardening efforts.

California and the southwestern United States has one of the most complex systems of weather conditions in the world. In a matter of a few city blocks, the weather can go from almost tropical, where bananas and papayas thrive, to grassy alpine meadows. The number of climatic areas within the state of California is reckoned in the dozens; local mini-climate variations can be counted in the hundreds.

The average temperature, rainfall, and amount of daily sunlight can change from one side of town to another or from the top of a hill to the valley two blocks away, from one side of a hill to the other.

As you have probably noticed from the performance of your local television weatherman, weather can be very unpredictable. In any locality, weather conditions vary greatly from hour to hour. A frosty morning can give way to a sunny, warm afternoon. Morning fog can clear into a beautiful blue sky, and that may develop into evening showers and thunderstorms.

About the only thing that can be discussed with any confidence is climate, the average temperature and rainfall for an area over a period of many years. It is on this long experience that you can make predictions about the seasons in a general area. As you might expect, climate, a matter of statistical probability, is a lot less chancy than day-to-day weather conditions. Thus, you will find yourself planning your gardening chores based on the climate in your area, but dealing with the more serious and immediate impact of the day-to-day weather.

When we discuss planning, it will be in terms of climate. Dealing with the practical work of gardening and the measures you must take to counter inclement conditions, we'll talk in terms of the weather. The one thing that you *can* count on, no matter where you live in California or the Southwest, is that it will be dry, especially during the summer months when your garden is growing. Only the few people who live halfway up a mountain get enough rain for their gardens. Almost anywhere else in the area, your plants will need watering.

Temperature

The same sort of quick changes in very short distances is also true of temperature. It can be cloudy and cool on the coast, hot and sunny a mile away, and cold in the mountains, all at the same time. Temperature will have a major impact on how you go about getting those vegetables to grow and your herbs tied up for drying.

Now, before all this makes the problem sound impossible, be assured that no matter how rugged the climate on your block, there are ways of getting your garden to grow without tremendous expense or long hours of work overcoming what the newscasters think of as ''natural disasters.''

If you are not especially set on what you want to grow in your garden, the easiest method of dealing with the weather is to plant the things that do well in your climate. To go this route, what you have to do is find out which vegetables and herbs grow best in your area and plant them. Later, in discussing specific vegetables and herbs,

Weather is a day-to-day matter; climate is the average of weather conditions over many years

we'll point out limitations on growing each, and we'll also suggest where you might look for further information if your individual problem seems to fall outside the pattern.

If, on the other hand, you know what you want and it does not coincide with local conditions, you will have to find ways of modifying the weather, at least around your plants. Again, we'll give you some practical help and advice later in this book.

Moisture

Although most gardeners begin to get the urge to start sticking seeds into the ground as the temperature begins to rise in the spring, moisture is by far a more important factor in gardening, especially in the desert or subtropical parts of the Southwest and California.

The clouds and soupy fogs that often invade the coastal areas do little to provide usable moisture to growing plants. Inland, the brilliant sun over the desert most of the year saps the last drop of moisture from the loose, sandy soil.

About all you can do to make sure enough water gets to your

plants is to irrigate them so that the roots have enough moisture. There are several ways to make sure the water you give the plants stays there, however, whether you bring water to them by trenches, by sprinkler, or by hose nozzle and watering can.

Protect your garden vegetables and herbs, if you live in an area where the wind may dry them out, by locating the garden in the lee of a building, by erecting fences that will act as a windbreak, or by planting trees or other heavy vegetation upwind from your garden plot. A fast-growing bamboo hedge, for example, may keep the wind from evaporating moisture almost as fast as you can add it.

If a windscreen cannot be accomplished, try planting your vegetables closer together than the recommended optimum distance. Plants give off water vapor as they breathe, and merely putting them close to each other will raise the humidity just above ground level.

A mulch of chopped wood, straw, shredded paper, or almost any inorganic substance will help hold in moisture if it is placed around plants in heavy layers. A mulch of loose consistency can, in fact, be used to cover young plants in danger of being dried out.

Mulches will also help when you are attempting to defend your plants from dazzling sun, as will practically any sort of shade.

When you are looking for shade, keep an eye out for areas that are already in the shadow of buildings, trees, or other plants. If there are no areas that will suit your purposes, you can always build a shading structure for the areas that need it. We will go into that in a later chapter.

One of the better ways to keep in humidity is to string a sheet of plastic just above the plants, in effect putting them in a temporary greenhouse. Not only is heat trapped by such an arrangement, but the moisture is kept from dissipating and the plants seem to bathe in high humidity. The only problem with this and other artificial shades is the need to build frames to hold them. This is a comparatively simple chore, as we'll see later.

One of the surest ways to keep the soil moist, in conjunction with the methods already discussed, is to water the plants in the cooler or calmer hours. If plants are watered in the evening or when

**Screen your vegetable plot from direct wind exposure.
Evaporation can occur very fast and be very damaging**

the wind is calm—which may be in the evening, too, in many areas—the water will have time to reach deeply into the soil before drying conditions return the next day.

A word of caution here. If you water so late that the leaves do not dry before the cool night arrives, you could be encouraging rot in stems and leaves. Some of the cool, damp areas of the California coast, for example, are notorious for plant rot and outdoor seedbeds that refuse to germinate. Also, be careful that your water does not hit the plants so hard that it damages them. Avoid touching the leaves of your plants when they are wet; it can encourage fungus growth.

Sunlight

Many areas of coastal California have the problem of too little sun. If you live in one of these foggier, cloudier places and you insist on growing plants that need sun, be prepared to make some adaptation.

17

You will probably have to start your plants indoors, try to locate them where they will receive a maximum amount of sunlight, consider planting at that time of year that will give the greatest amount of natural sunlight, if other conditions permit, and make sure you keep the plants warm.

Warmth

Besides sunlight and moisture, your plants will need warmth if they are to make the feast you want from them. For the vast majority of vegetables, which are annuals, that means they will have to be planted at a time early in the year when they are safe from killing frost and will have to be harvested before the frost returns in the fall.

The few perennial plants among the vegetables, such as artichoke, rhubarb, asparagus, cardoon, and shallots, can be planted either in the spring, after the last low temperature threat, or in the early fall, as long as they have time to get well established before the chill returns to the air.

None of this means, however, that vegetable gardening is limited purely to a summer occupation. In many parts of California, the weather is warm enough for vegetables to grow throughout the year.

It is also true that you are able to choose between plants that will do well only in hot weather and those that cannot survive midsummer heat. If careful scheduling is part of your garden plan, you can be growing cool weather vegetables in the early spring and fall, with the hot weather crops coming in between.

The gardener in most parts of California and the Southwest is fortunate that television and radio stations are highly sensitive to the chance of frost. They can be counted on to give advance warning when the temperature is expected to threaten crops. Weather advisories may be issued for the protection of the massive citrus groves of Southern California or the economically important commercial farms of the Central Valley, but the information they contain is the same the home gardener needs to protect his plot.

A heavy mulching is one of the best ways of helping your plants retain their heat. Old bedsheets, polyethylene film, newspapers,

Hot caps: one of the best ways of protecting plants from frost damage

tarpaulins, mattress pads, or practically anything spread above the plants for the night will help them stay warm. Cardboard boxes set over the plants will protect them from frost, as will hot caps—small cones made from waxed paper. The smudge pot, depending on the wind and other weather factors, may or may not be a feasible method of bringing heat to a small area like a kitchen garden.

In this instance too, as with maintaining a high moisture content in the air, planting vegetables closer together than usually recommended will be an advantage. They will keep each other warm to some extent.

A string of 100-watt light bulbs suspended about a foot above the plants—the distance between bulbs will depend on conditions in your particular plot and you should seek extension or garden shop help—a burning charcoal brazier, or recently developed oil-impregnated combustible bricks will all help protect tender plants from a really cold night.

Some gardeners report good results from the ancient practice of spraying a fine water mist over their plants as the temperature drops below freezing. Nobody is sure who tried this first, but it has been successful in some of the Southern California citrus groves. Apparently the mist freezing on the plants insulates them against even colder air. The misting procedure also has the added advantage of permitting the plants to thaw slowly after a freeze. The principle will be familiar to those coming from colder areas: a blanket of snow protects plants that would otherwise be exposed to much greater degrees of cold from the air itself, since snow or ice will remain very close to the 32°F freezing point of water.

19

The problem with these last methods, however, is that they all require special equipment. If you have not purchased the equipment in advance so that it is at hand, it is too late when the weatherman issues his warning and all the shops are closed. In addition to providing you with the right tools at the right time, planning can give you a decided edge in protecting your plants from frosty nights.

In areas where there is risk of early or late frost damaging plants, the gardener should plant in an open area or on high ground when he can. Cold air is heavier than hot air and tends to collect in low spots and in yards surrounded by solid fences; it also remains in such places longer since it has nowhere to go but up and must be considerably heated to rise.

But don't let the fact that you live at the bottom of a valley stop your gardening plans; just be ready with whatever is needed to deal with chilly nights when and if they come.

If there is a south-facing slope on your land, put your garden on it if there is any chance of cold damage. If not, attempt to arrange the plot so the cold-hardy plants are in the cooler spots—usually the lowest points—and the sun-lovers are in the warmer parts of the garden. Remember that winds moving down a slope are warming winds and that, erosion possibilities aside, a hillside may be one of the best places for your garden. Terracing—establishing a level area on a hillside—may be a possibility on a not-too-steep hill.

The overhanging eaves of buildings, the lee side of structures, and overhanging tree branches will all defend tender plants from frost to some extent. If you decide to make use of such protection, be sure you remember that trees and other large plants send out roots for long distances and that they may compete with your vegetables for moisture and food; they may also provide too much shade for sun-loving plants.

To sum up, success in dealing with the weather is most often simply a matter of knowing what to expect and being prepared to deal with it.

2 Soil

Once you are ready to deal with the trials of the weather, you can begin learning to deal with the soil. Here, as with the weather, scientists may spend a lifetime comprehending what happens in the ground when things grow, but you can get the knowledge of soil chemistry you need with a lot less effort.

The soil of your garden is composed of three distinct layers: the topsoil, which contains most of the decaying vegetation and animal matter that provides plant food, as well as most of the bacteria, fungi, and insects; the subsoil, often heavy in iron oxides and other salts washed out of the topsoil; and the bedrock that will seldom have much significance for you.

Basically, you will have to be concerned with five soil factors if your vegetables and herbs are to produce: minerals, decaying organic matter, water, air, and the worms, insects, and other small and microscopic life in the ground. An imbalance in any of these can spell trouble for your crop unless you are aware of it and can deal with it.

Obtaining a soil sample is a simple procedure

Soil tests

The first thing you should do when you decide to start a garden is have the soil tested. The pH test is a complicated chemical comparison of hydrogen particles in the soil, but it will tell you all you need to know of the acid condition of your ground.

To get your test sample, clear the debris from the soil and take samples from about three inches below the surface in at least fifteen different spots. Each sample should be approximately tablespoon size. One good way to get the samples is to stick a spade in the ground, then push the blade forward, exposing a cut. Dig the sample out of the side of the cut and put it into a jar, a plastic bag, or any similar container. Don't worry about keeping the samples separated; the chemical test will be for the whole plot.

Once you have the sample, take it to your county agricultural agent, who will send it to a laboratory for testing. In many areas the test is free.

The result for your plot will come back as a number between 4 and 9. The best finding for a garden is 6 or 7. The lower your soil's pH, the more acid it is. The higher numbers mean it is alkaline. A pH of 7 is neutral, neither acid nor alkaline, the score a sample of river water (unpolluted) would make. Often the result will be accompanied by the chemist's suggestions for improving your soil for a good garden.

If you want to do your own testing, there are do-it-yourself soil test kits available. Follow the directions and you will get a pretty good idea of the condition of your soil. It will not be as precise, however, as the evaluation of a chemist working under laboratory conditions.

If your ground is too acid, a condition that is common in rainy areas with sandy soil, you have to add lime. Follow the chemist's recommendations on how much to use and which type—ground or hydrated—is best for your soil. Hydrated lime usually works faster, but it does not last as long as the ground kind.

You can lime your garden at any time, but it is best to do it in the spring or fall. Ground lime can be put on with your fertilizer, but there should be a week's interval between applications of hydrated lime and fertilizer.

Applying lime to your garden gives your plants a good dose of calcium and magnesium. If your ground has a lot of clay, the lime will improve drainage, aeration, and the development of beneficial organisms.

Alkalinity—the presence of too much lime and other minerals—is common in rain-free areas like Southern California and the Southwest. This condition, indicated by a pH of more than 7, makes life hard for most garden plants.

About the only practical measures you can take to minimize alkaline soil are practicing careful watering techniques, discussed later, and avoiding unnecessary cultivation. Add plenty of humus—organic matter—to the topsoil and level the ground to eliminate points where salts may concentrate. Mixing gypsum or sulfur with the topsoil can aid a bad alkaline condition, but you should apply it only with the advice of your county agent or an experienced garden shop operator.

Most of the urban Southwest has grown up on river floodplains or terraces. With irrigation, the soil, which originated as silty deposits, becomes extremely fertile. But you should be prepared for a whole range of problems that could be present in your soil.

Salinity is an excess of salt in the soil, common in arid and semi-arid regions. It can stop plant germination, stunt your plant's growth, burn its foliage, and may even kill it. You can temporarily ease this acid condition with heavy occasional watering.

Another difficulty you may encounter is chlorosis, a shortage of iron that makes itself known by the yellowing of the leaf surfaces between the veins. This can be corrected with applications of iron sulfate or a number of other iron compounds.

Deficiencies in nitrogen, phosphorus, or potassium can be overcome through additions of fertilizers. Manure or finely ground compost are also helpful to some degree and aid in building up the humus in the soil.

If your topsoil is shallow and the subsoil has developed into hardpan, vegetable and herb roots will be blocked from growing as deeply as they should, and the drainage will be poor. You may be able to counter this condition by breaking up the hardpan if it isn't too thick. If it is, however, your best bet is to move the garden to another spot or build raised beds for the plants.

The problem hardpan creates may require installation of a drainage system. However, this can be expensive and might not solve your problems if the hardpan layer blocks root growth.

The principal, if not the only, point of bringing up these potential soil problems you may encounter is to insure that you are aware that they exist. Most of them can be solved without tremendous effort if you know that they are there.

If you have any doubts about your soil's ability to support a garden after the results of the pH test, you might want to have a C/N analysis done. This test, performed by your county agent, will tell you the proportion of carbon and nitrogen, both of them essential elements, in your soil.

Assuming your test does not turn up any serious shortages of either element, the results can still tell you a lot about how to fertilize your particular soil by indicating which fertilizer balance will give you the results you want. In a later chapter we'll talk about the contents of various fertilizers.

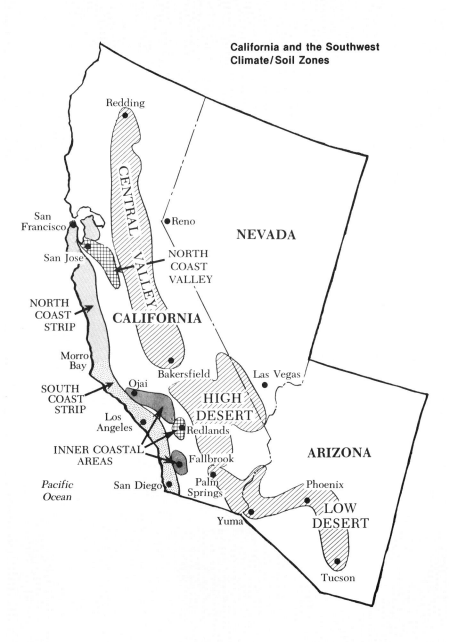

California and the Southwest Climate/Soil Zones

Redding

San Francisco

San Jose

CENTRAL VALLEY

Reno

NORTH COAST VALLEY

NEVADA

NORTH COAST STRIP

CALIFORNIA

Morro Bay

SOUTH COAST STRIP

Ojai

Bakersfield

Las Vegas

HIGH DESERT

Los Angeles

INNER COASTAL AREAS

Redlands

ARIZONA

Fallbrook

Pacific Ocean

San Diego

Palm Springs

Phoenix

LOW DESERT

Yuma

Tucson

Soil texture

Now, before you stick your spade in the ground, you need to know something about the soil's texture. Sandy desert soils are easy to cultivate because they are loose and grainy. But they are poor water holders, and much watering will quickly wash away whatever nutrients they hold.

In non-desert areas you may find yourself faced with adobe clay so hard you need a jackhammer to cut furrows. These heavy clay soils hold nutrients but they swell up when they get damp, and they are so compact that they block drainage and air movement.

Your soil will probably fall somewhere between these two extremes. And with a little luck, your garden plot will be on one of the vast alluvial deposits left by an ancient river. You may have one of those slightly clayey soils with enough sand to permit easy cultivation, allow good drainage, and hold their nutrients. The odds are, however, that your ground will tend toward one of the extremes and you will have to bring it into a balance that will support your plants.

You have a lot of help in this battle if you only know where to find it. One of your greatest allies is the earthworm, whose main value lies in digging up the ground from below. As worms burrow through the soil, usually from about 6 inches deep down to several feet, they break up the soil and neutralize its acidity with their body fluids. Worm digging lets in air vital for plant growth and allows water to soak in more easily.

Worms that aerate the soil and neutralize its acidity are allies of the gardener

Some experienced gardeners credit earthworms with doubling the growth of their plants and their crop production. Whether that is true or not, earthworms are certainly a good indicator of a plot's condition. They will avoid ground that is too acid or too alkaline.

Preparation

Usually, you should begin preparation of a new garden plot in the fall before the first spring planting. Using a spade or a spading fork, turn the ground, burying whatever vegetation is growing on it. This will expose to the air and kill many of the insects and disease germs that may be waiting to damage your vegetables. If you wait too late to break your ground in the fall and it freezes hard with the onset of winter, this turning can be done in the early spring. In either case, you should go over the ground with a spading fork and a hoe, and later a rake, until it is worked into pieces fine enough so that it rakes smooth.

One word of caution: if your soil is clayey, don't dig when it is wet. The soil will stick in large lumps to your spade or fork, making very heavy labor with little results. Cultivating wet clay will also pack the soil particles closer together, making bad drainage even worse and shutting out air. It will dry into chunks with the consistency of well-set concrete.

Experienced gardeners have long argued over how much the soil should be cultivated. Some are constantly digging, hoeing, or raking, while others contend that distributing the soil any more than absolutely necessary destroys organic matter and ruins the ground.

Since both sides can show outstanding examples of gardening success to prove their point, what you do is up to you once you get your ground ready for planting. Just make sure you do enough to keep the weeds down.

About all you have to remember is that heavy cultivation has a tendency to shake the plant nutrients out of loose sandy soil, leaving mineral conditions you don't want.

When clayey soil is dry, hoeing, which is the equivalent of the tilling that the farmer gives his ground, helps to get air into the tight soil. Another way you can improve the drainage and aeration of clayey soil is to mix it with sand or crushed rock to about 2 feet deep. Organic matter added to the ground will usually help build up humus, but you should think twice before adding it to relatively sterile sandy ground. Certainly, anything that helps build up humus in sand is desirable. But keep in mind that too much aeration is the reason organic matter decays and loses its value so rapidly in sandy ground. When you add a soil amendment, you speed up aeration.

Your way around this dilemma is to add a slow-decaying amendment, such as peat moss, ground-up tree bark, sawdust, or such organic matter as the spent hops from the local brewery. A check with your local garden shop operator or county agent, or with experienced gardeners in your neighborhood, will give you some idea of which soil additives seem to produce the best results in your area.

If you decide you need a soil amendment, be sure you get a C/N test before you pick one. To get any results from an amendment, you have to add an amount equaling at least half the volume of the soil needing help. Thus, to get results in 100 cubic feet of ground, you will need to add 50 to 100 cubic feet of the amendment.

Leaves, peat moss, and garden compost almost always have sufficient nitrogen to support their own decomposition. But fresh sawdust, evergreen needles, and some other additives will deplete the nitrogen in the soil as they decompose. If you already have a nitrogen shortage in your garden plot and add the wrong material, you can make matters worse. The C/N test is easy to get and it can save you from an expensive mistake.

On the whole, the available tests, a little advice from people who know what they are talking about, your efforts, and strict adherence to the old adage about moderation in all things should get you the kind of soil you need to grow vegetables and herbs.

3 Seeds or Seedlings

There are several ways you can start plants. Cuttings, layering, budding, division, or grafting can all be used to carry plants over from one season to another. But for vegetables and herbs, you will usually be using seeds or seedlings for your stock.

If you are lucky, you are not one of those gardeners who buys his garden stock on the spur of the moment when he happens to pass a seed rack. The impulse buyer often buys because of the colorful pictures on a seed packet and never reads the information on the back of the pack. If this describes you, you could be asking for unnecessary troubles.

Always get your garden stock from a reliable source. Many seed varieties do not produce well when they have been stored for more than a year. Others may be from hybrid stock or an accidental hybrid mixture that will not produce well at all. If these seeds do produce a plant, the odds are it may not resemble its parents in some perhaps essential respects.

In modern America, you can easily forget that seeds come from plants, not out of a factory. Nature designed seeds to germinate and grow in natural surroundings. Under natural conditions, they fall from the parent plant and lie among the leaves and other ground debris in surroundings that permitted the parent plant to grow, flower, and form seed. Even then a long time may pass before the seeds sprout and the plants start growing. They survive through all sorts of temperature and moisture changes. Putting such seeds into an artificial environment can often halt their ability to germinate and produce a worthwhile plant.

This is one of the reasons it is a good idea to begin your garden with seedlings. You save time, you do not have to go through all the preliminaries sometimes necessary to start seeds, and you know you are going to have plants.

If you cannot get seedlings or if you want to start from scratch, you must know what preparations are necessary before the seeds go into the ground.

Seeds

Fleshy seeds, such as beans, sometimes develop a hard skin or outer crust if they have been stored for a while. Soak them in tepid water for at least a day to soften their cover before planting or they may not germinate. It may be necessary to chip or file the coating of hard-coated seeds—on the opposite side from the seed's eye—before they are planted, or moisture may not get to the seed germ and it will lie dormant for a long time.

Other vegetable seeds are oily when they drop from the plant. If you store them in a warm spot, they will dry out. Shrivelled seeds may not germinate and it is usually a bad idea to keep such seeds for more than one season.

Beyond these brief cautions, about all you can do to make sure you are getting good seeds is buy them from a reputable dealer or catalog, make sure the packets are dated so you know how old they are, and buy strains bred to resist the insects, diseases, and adverse elements in your area. By and large, do not try to save your own seeds. Many modern vegetable strains are hybrids and their seeds will sprout plants randomly showing the characteristics of the ancestors.

As a general rule you can count on hybrids to produce better, stronger plants than standard strains. But you should get detailed information from an experienced garden shop operator or your county agent before you make a final decision on a seed strain.

Of all the ways you can start plants, the chanciest is from seeds you saved from earlier seasons. You have no guarantee that seeds from a vigorous, top-producing plant will grow in the same way as its parent. The controlled conditions for fertilizing and cross-fertilizing that exist in commercial seed farms just do not exist in the home garden.

As was said earlier, hybrid seeds seldom if ever produce true to the parent plants. The same kind of problem of differing strains can develop in standard varieties grown in your own plot if they have accidentally become cross-pollinated, that is, pollinated from a plant of a different and perhaps modifying strain, and there is no way to be sure about it until it may be too late.

Even if your plot is a long way from your neighbor's, it is vulnerable to cross-pollination. Most seed experts believe a quarter of a mile spacing is the minimum to guard against cross-pollination. For corn or other crops that are pollinated by bees or the wind, the required spacing may be as much as half a mile.

Seedlings

If you decide to start your vegetables from seedlings, what you should do is to look for a rich, green plant that appears healthy. The pots or flats in which it is growing should contain moist soil and the plant itself should have good leafage and be well-rounded, not thin and spindly.

Seedlings should not be over-delicate and should have good root systems

The great plus value about starting with seedlings is that the reputable nursery will not have put them on sale until it is normally time for them to take their places in the outdoor garden, both in terms of the season of the year and of the development of the plants.

If you prefer, you can establish a garden by planting seeds directly in the ground. Direct planting will save you the chore of transplanting from the seedling flats, and it will sometimes give you healthier plants than those you get if you start them indoors and move them later. Although starting your seeds indoors in pots or flats will give you a lot more plants for the number of seeds you use, putting the seeds directly where they will grow in the garden, from the beginning, will save you a lot of effort. It is a good method for those hardy, fast-growing plants best adapted to conditions in your area.

Planting

The most common way to plant vegetables and herbs is in furrows or hills. A hill to a gardener is not necessarily a heaped-up bit of ground, but rather a place where a group of seeds has been planted. How far apart the seeds or seedlings should be spaced or how many should be in each hill depends on the specific plant. Another planting method you can use with some herbs is broadcasting—scattering seeds uniformly throughout a marked-off area.

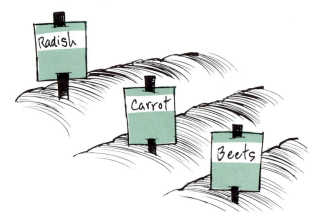

Mark the furrows after planting. It is easy to forget what is planted in any particular place, even in a small garden

Once they are in place, you should cover the seeds with earth from a quarter to two inches deep, depending on the size of the seed itself. Generally, you should cover seeds to a depth about twice their diameter. It may be deeper in very sandy soil or shallower in heavy clays. Pack the soil gently once the seeds are covered and, if the ground is dry, give the plot a light watering. The idea is to permit the opening seed to establish its root system and get its leaves into the air and light.

Don't forget to mark your rows or hills so you'll know what you've planted. Otherwise, if you have a memory lapse, you might have to wait until they sprout to see what you have—and even then you might not know unless you can tell one seed leaf from another.

Indoor planting is a good method for seeds you want to give an early start or for extremely small seeds, as well as for those that take a long time to germinate. It has the advantage of letting you control the amount of light, shade, and moisture the seeds receive during the most delicate time of their growth. As with seedlings, beginning seeds indoors will also save you a lot of thinning later.

Starting Seeds

There are many types of containers you can get in which to start seeds. Traditional nursery flats are the most common. They are shallow boxes, about 3 inches deep and usually a foot wide by a foot and a half long. The bottom boards are separated so excess water can drain. In addition to flats, seeds can be planted in a variety of pots, pans, cut-off milk cartons, or even on glass or paper sheets. You can get tiny pots made of compressed peat moss or manure that have the added advantage of going into the ground with the young plant, thus avoiding the shock of transplanting. Seed-starter kits also are available. These contain seeds, humus, and nutrients; all you do is take off the lid and add water.

If you decide to use new clay pots for your seeds, be sure to soak them in water as they will draw a lot of moisture from the soil if filled when dry. Whatever your container, make sure it is clean and there is an opening in the bottom for drainage.

The containers in which to start seeds are everywhere

You will find a variety of soil or artificial mixtures and soil recipes available to fill your containers. If you use soil, make it about two-thirds loose, sandy topsoil and a third peat moss or a crumbled leaf-mold-and-sand mixture. Another recipe calls for equal parts of sand, peat moss or finely ground tree bark, and sifted topsoil.

To keep down damping-off disease, steam your mixture thoroughly by baking it in the oven or drenching it with a good commercial fungicide before it is used. Damping-off disease is a variety of deadly stem-rot fungus that spreads when there is too much moisture and not enough air circulation around young plants. It can get started merely because the developing shoots are too close together.

Components of a good potting soil, which is shown in
center. From the top, reading clockwise, sand, leaf
mold, fir shavings, perlite, peat moss

You may want to sow your vegetable seeds in one of the sterile
soil substitutes currently on the market. Vermiculite, ground-up
sphagnum moss, or perlite can be used alone or mixed. Redi-Earth,
Cornell Mix, and Jiffy Mix are three of these soil substitutes plus
fertilizer which are said to do the job very well.

Fill your containers with the soil or soil mixture three-quarters
to half an inch from the top, then firm the soil with gentle pressure.

Pencil used to mark a small furrow for the larger seeds

For large seeds, cut furrows or drill lines of holes about 2 inches apart in the soil with a small instrument. A pencil or pointed piece of lath will work well.

Put the seeds in about an inch and a half apart and cover them with a layer of soil approximately equal to their diameter. Very fine seeds can be spread on top of the soil, pressed in with your palm, and covered with a very thin layer of soil. Put only one variety of seed in a container.

It is a good idea to dust your seeds with a good fungicide before planting them.

Once you have watered the flats lightly, cover them with clear plastic food wrap, paper, burlap, or a glass pane. Keep the flats out of direct sunlight in a spot where the temperature can be maintained between 60 and 70 degrees F, and keep them watered. In a few days, when the first leaves are out, uncover the flats and move them into the light.

If you put them near a window for sunlight, the plants will grow toward the light source. Be sure to turn the flats periodically to insure uniform development.

Some authorities contend that you should forget about sunlight altogether. The light through a normal window simply is not enough to help young plants, they argue. These gardeners suggest you use a 48-inch fluorescent light fixture that has two or more daylight or cool white tubes. Hang the light about a foot above your flats, leave it burning around the clock, they say, and it will give you all the light necessary for vigorous plants.

The first greenery you will see in your flats will be the so-called "seed leaves." When the plants develop their first "true" leaves— the first leaves the plant will keep through the season—thin and transplant the seedlings. Dig out the individual seedlings carefully with a blunt knife, lifting them, but not pulling them, by their leaves and putting them into a freshly prepared flat. Try to keep as much soil as possible around the plant's root system. The new flat should be filled with a slightly coarser soil or soil substitute mixture. Press the soil gently around the roots so that the plant is firm, water it well, and give the seedling a light dose of liquid fertilizer. The plants should be spaced about 2 inches apart, with approximately 3 to 4 inches between rows.

Once the plants have the space they need to continue their development, you can begin the hardening-off process—getting them ready for outdoor exposure.

Some gardeners prefer to give the seedlings a couple of days to get over the shock of transplanting before they are progressively exposed to outdoor conditions. The first day set the flats outdoors in a sunny spot, sheltered from the wind, for an hour or two. Increase the amount of time the plants are left outside each day until they are out around the clock. You must give your seedlings protection from hard winds and frost, but once they have stayed out for a full twenty-four hours, don't bring them back in no matter how bad the weather.

Cold frames

Another hardening-off method used by some gardeners is to move the pots or flats into cold frames as soon as the seedlings have been transplanted. A cold frame is basically a wooden box built on the

A cold frame planting bed for starting seedlings

ground that acts in some ways like a greenhouse. It has a glass or transparent lid that provides protection for tender young plants while exposing them to at least a moderate form of outdoor garden conditions.

Cold frames are used by some gardeners to start their seeds. If you plant seeds or transplant your seedlings into a cold frame, build up a 3-inch layer of gravel to aid drainage. Another 3- or 4-inch layer of soil or soil substitute should be built over the gravel if you intend to plant in the cold frame. The gravel bed can be used as the base for flats or pots if the cold frame is used for hardening-off.

Seeds started in a cold frame will develop more slowly than if begun indoors and cannot be planted as early in the year. Fumigate the soil, give it a treatment of balanced fertilizer, and keep it watered and weeded.

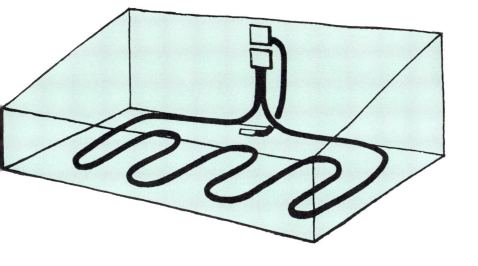

The cold frame can become a hot bed with the addition of a heating element and insulation

Put seeds in the frame in rows about 6 inches apart and thin them when they develop a couple of sets of true leaves. You can cover the top of the cold frame with mulch, blankets, or practically anything else that insulates to keep out the cold on frosty nights. In especially cold climates, an electric heating cable can be installed in the ground under the frame, or a 100-watt incandescent bulb can be put in, and the cold frame becomes a hot bed.

You harden-off cold-frame or hot-bed seedlings by opening the lid a little more each day until the box is open around the clock.

You will find a detailed discussion of cold frames and hot beds in Chapter VII, ''Artificial Environments.''

If you use a hot bed, be sure to lower the temperature of the heating element when you begin to harden-off the seedlings.

When your hardened-off seedlings have grown to the point

where the leaves begin to overlap those of neighboring plants, they should be ready for transplanting into your garden plot.

The proper time for starting seeds depends almost entirely on the weather in your area and the kind of vegetables and herbs you are planning to grow. You should discuss the question with your garden shop operator or county agent as soon as you have selected the varieties and strains you intend to use. This may seem like a small matter, but it is best not to hold back your plants by leaving them in containers when they are ready to go into the ground.

As we stated earlier, one way to avoid many of these chores is to buy seedlings when they are available. It will save you most of this procedure except the hardening-off. The companies selling seedlings have taken care of the soil mix and the thinning, and they usually offer plants adapted to the area in which they are sold. The plants are also put on the market at the right time for planting, so even the hardening-off process is minimized, if not eliminated. But since they have usually been kept in the controlled environment of a nursery building, seedlings should still be hardened-off before they are put into the ground. The nursery has done the rest of the work for you.

4 *Vegetables*

When you first approach the seed catalogs or the seed packets and seedling racks in your garden shop, you will find a wide variety of plants within each category. But, despite the dizzying array of vegetables available, there will be probably only a few major varieties you will want on your dining table.

There are all sorts of lettuce, for example, and several apparently identical radishes, and a monumental number of beans. You can avoid a lot of confusion, however, if you keep in mind that the different plant varieties are either the result of adaptation to different climates or soil conditions over the years or they were laboratory-created to cope with specific diseases or climatic extremes. You can eliminate considering most of them and concentrate only on those adapted for your area.

In general, you can expect vegetables to be hardy feeders needing plenty of moisture and sunlight to produce. Skimping on either water or light may check plant growth. Many vegetables are full-draft plants that need plenty of soil depth to grow, but others can be damaged by deep cultivation because their roots are so shallow.

This chapter is designed to provide you with essential information for putting your vegetables into your garden plot either as seeds or seedlings.

Legumes include the many varieties of beans

LEGUMES (beans and peas) are some of the most common vegetables. Beans are generally a hot weather crop; and if you plant them in soil that is too cold or too dense, they may not sprout. Plant beans in warm weather and only after any heavy soil has been reconditioned.

Green beans, often called snap beans, are a stringless variety grown either as bush or pole crops for their fleshy pods rather than for the beans themselves. Although both types will produce well, the pole variety will give you more crop for the space available.

Pole beans can be strung up on a pole planted next to them, or they can be attached to a nearby trellis, a fence, or a hill of corn. They will climb almost anything.

You should plant either green or pole beans in well-fertilized ground. Rows of bush beans should be approximately 18 inches apart with furrows approximately 2 inches deep. Bean seeds should be planted about 3 inches apart in the row and covered an inch or two deep, depending on the soil consistency. Gently firm the ground above the seeds to aid germination.

If the soil is extremely heavy, you might consider covering the

42

beans with a mixture of sand, humus, and peat rather than with soil.

If you are planting seedlings, whether you bought them or sprouted your seeds indoors, plant them about 4 to 6 inches apart. If you start with seeds in the furrows, thin them to the same spacing when the plants get 2 to 4 inches high. When your plants are about a foot tall, you can encourage a heavy yield by giving them a good top dressing of fertilizer. Top dressing is, of course, a matter simply of spreading the food without mixing it into the topsoil.

About this time, bank the soil 3 or 4 inches deep around the plants. It helps keep in the moisture, discourages weeds, and gives the plants a good cultivation.

You plant and cultivate pole beans like green beans but in a circle of five or six plants around the pole. Keep the poles at least 3 feet apart.

If the beans are planted along a fence or trellis, place them approximately 6 inches apart when they first go into the ground. Once the beans have gotten a good start, they should be thinned so that no more than 2 or 3 plants are climbing each pole.

One bit of knowledge that will save you a lot of trouble in keeping your pole beans where they belong is to remember that their tendrils twine clockwise as they grow upward. Start them in that direction and they won't be falling off all the time.

Lima beans are planted and cultivated much the same way as green and pole beans, but you should not plant them until the ground has had a chance to get warm. You can get both small and large lima beans in either bush or pole varieties.

The long pod fava—also called the English broad or green-shell bean—is grown much like its relatives but it is hardier. It can be substituted for the other beans in cooler climates and can be planted earlier than the rest.

Peas, unlike their bean cousins, are cool weather crops. Plant them in fast-draining but moisture-retaining soil in the early spring. Normal-sized peas are usually grown on supports, since the vines get to be as much as 6 feet long. Dwarf peas, however, grow only 15 inches to 2 feet high and need no support.

Plant your peas in double rows with 3 or 4 inches between them. The plants should be about 2 inches apart. Put a couple of feet between the sets of double rows. Once the plants are about 9 inches high, a small amount of fertilizer should be placed next to them. Cultivate only enough to keep the weeds out.

One of the most common pea varieties is the edible-pod or sugar pea, often called the snow pea. When these peas are young, just as the peas in the pod are becoming lumps, they have the fleshy quality of snap beans and are cooked in the same manner. Let them age and you shell them before they are prepared.

Plant cowpeas—black-eyed peas or Southern table peas—after all danger of frost is gone. Their furrows should be approximately 2 inches deep with seeds or plants 2 to 4 inches apart. Thin them to 4 or more inches between plants when they reach a height of 3 inches. Put your rows 3 or 4 feet apart and keep the surface soil cultivated and weed-free.

Do not handle or cultivate peas or beans when they are damp as such treatment could injure the plants.

EDIBLE ROOTS found in the garden include carrots, turnips and rutabagas, beets, parsnips, radishes, and salsify. Though they are all roots that are eaten, they belong to different families.

Carrots and parsnips are members of the parsley family. Radishes and turnips are mustards. Salsify is a daisy (a composite), and beets belong to the goosefoot family.

Plant all of them as early in the spring as possible. These plants grow best when it is cool and a lot of heat will hurt their quality.

Before they go into the ground, treat the area in which they will be planted with a band of synthetic fertilizer beside the rows. This method of applying fertilizer, beside the plant rows where it can reach the roots, is called side-dressing. If you prefer, well-aged manure can be blended into the topsoil in place of the side-dressing.

Carrot seeds germinate unevenly and should be sown heavily—30 or more seeds per foot of row. They need loose soil above them that is kept constantly moist for best results. When the carrot tops are about 2 inches high, thin them to about 1½ inches between plants. If you start your seeds indoors, set the seedlings out the same distance apart. Apply another light commercial fertilizer side-dressing near the rows at about this time, too.

Parsnips and salsify are cultivated much like their carrot cousins. Plant salsify deep in rich, sandy soil for best results.

If you are faced with heavy soil and a strong yen for carrots, parsnips, or salsify, consider planting these root vegetables in an artificial sand trench. You may also want to consider growing one of the short, fat varieties of carrot, such as Oxheart or French Forcing, so the heavy soil is not such a serious factor.

Plant turnips and rutabagas in late winter for spring harvest, in midsummer for fall harvest, or in the fall for late winter harvest in mild winter areas.

Sow your turnips in shallow furrows with seeds spread thin. Cover them with less than an inch of soil and thin them to a couple of inches apart when the plants come up. If you start the seeds indoors or use seedlings, space them when you plant. Another way of planting turnips is to broadcast the seeds and then rake them into the soil.

Rutabaga culture is basically the same as for turnips.

The flavor of both these plants improves with a touch of cold

Root vegetables such as radishes and carrots form one of the important vegetable crops

weather, and therefore they can be planted before many of your other vegetables go outside.

You will find that beets are one of the most weather-versatile plants. They are adaptable to both heat and cold and can be planted up to a month before the final frost-free day in chilly areas. Put them into inch-deep furrows, about 3 inches apart, and cover with an inch of soil. Space the rows approximately 18 inches apart.

When your plants are about 2 inches tall, thin them to maintain their 3-inch spacing, and when they are about 6 inches, put on a top-dressing fertilizer. Beets should be put into friable (easily crumbled) soil with plenty of nutrients.

Beets, though grown principally for the sweet edible root, also have delicious leafage. Swiss chard is, in fact, a beet especially adapted for its greens. Leaf growth is encouraged by use of nitrogen-rich fertilizers, but any complete plant food will give you edible beet greens.

As long as your soil is friable, rich, and moist, it will grow radishes. Mix a little fertilizer with the soil, put the radish seeds in furrows, and cover with a thin layer of soil, about a quarter of an inch deep. Radishes will grow to eating size in a very few days and can be planted in both the spring and fall.

Radishes can be grown, as every gardener knows, between rows in vegetable beds, among the flowers of a flower bed, even as an edging along a garden walk. Plant them in various locations a week apart, or even twice a week, and you can have radishes at every meal from mid-spring to late autumn.

CORN is the only cereal grain normally grown in the garden. Sweet corn can be raised almost anywhere there is plenty of heat in the summer, but you will find these tall plants most suitable if you have a large garden plot.

To get the best from your corn crop, put the plants 6 to 8 inches apart in rows, or in hills (groups of 4 to 6 seeds), 2 or 3 feet apart. Your rows must be at least 2 feet apart if you are going to get the pollination necessary for ears to form. The best arrangement is to

Corn requires room to grow in rows spaced properly to insure pollination. It may not be suitable for the very small garden plot.

plant 4 rows at an angle to the prevailing wind. And, of course, one row planted so that the wind blows at right angles will result in nothing at all.

Remember, also, that there are varieties of corn that grow to from 4 to 8 feet tall, so plant your corn where it won't shade the other parts of your garden plot. Again, it is most important to read your seed packet to know just what it is you are planting.

Your corn planting must wait until all risk of frost has passed and the ground has started to warm up. Keep the weeds out of the rows and add a top dressing when the plants are about a foot high. If you mound the soil around the growing plants, it will help keep down weeds and cover up the prop roots. The prop roots, or suckers, don't weaken the plant or its yield, so in general leave them alone.

If you want to experiment a bit, think of growing popcorn, or multicolored Indian corn for late fall decoration.

VINES yield two garden crops. These two—squashes and cucumbers—cannot stand any frost. They suck up nutrients at a tremendous rate, so add a shovel of manure when you plant them. Note that these vines need either a lot of space in which to spread or something on which to climb upward. If your garden area is limited,

47

don't plant too many of these vine seeds. Also, there are some bush varieties you may be able to find.

Plant both summer and winter squash—winter squash has a hard rind, summer squash is picked before it is mature and is eaten rind and all—3 or 4 seeds or sets in hills about 4 feet apart. When the plants start growing, thin out all but two or three of the best ones in each hill. Winter squashes take 3 or 4 months to ripen because of their hard shell; however, summer sqaush, such as zucchini, will ripen in about 2 months.

An extra attraction are the edible squash blossoms. Since the female flowers produce the fruit, pick only the male blossoms. Stuffed and fried, these are tasty snacks or hors d'oeuvres.

Plant cucumbers with a heavy dose of fertilizer or manure nearby, but not directly contacting the seeds. One of the best methods you can use to insure proper feeding of cucumbers is to remove a bucket of soil, mix it with a bucket of well-rotted manure, and replace it in the hole. Put another bucket of soil on top of the mix and plant the seeds 4 inches from the fertilized soil. Put 6 or more seeds in each hill and thin to 3 when the plants are growing. If you start seeds indoors, plant 3 seedlings to a hill.

It is a good idea to provide a tripod, a trellis, or a fence for these prolific vines to climb.

BULBS include the onion and its relatives, one of the easiest crops you can grow, as they thrive in a wide variety of climatic and soil conditions. They have a strong tolerance for cold weather and are resistant to heat too. These plants are best begun from sets, or small bulbs, rather than from seed.

For best results, put your onions in well-drained, rich soil, free of stones, clods, or trash. The sets should be in 2-inch furrows about 2 inches deep, with approximately a pound of well-rotted manure spread for every square foot of ground. Also add about 5 pounds of commercial fertilizer to each 100 square feet of onion plot.

Once the onion sets start to grow, thin them to about 4 inches between plants. Just pull up the excess and eat them.

Acorn squash. Squashes are a vine crop and all are good eating and fun to grow

Onions are the principal bulb crop in the home garden

You can space your onion rows anywhere from 6 to 15 inches apart and still get good results. Cultivate between rows to keep down the weeds. Work a little chicken manure into the soil between rows to hold up the ground's nitrogen content while your onions grow. Take care when you cultivate your onion plot; they are shallow plants and are easily injured.

The shallot, a mild, sweet onion, should be grown like any other onion. Put your sets 6 to 10 inches apart and fertilize once or twice while they grow. Unlike onions, which are usually planted in the spring, your shallots go in in the fall and develop through the winter.

Start garlic by breaking the bulb into its individual cloves and planting the pieces, base down, 2 or 3 inches apart and an inch or two deep.

The leek is a close relative of the onion but does not form a bulb. These long-stalked plants, grown for their edible leaves, are started from seeds. Sown approximately a quarter of an inch deep and cultivated much like onions, they will grow into stalks approximately 18 inches long. To get mild, white leeks, blanch them by drawing the earth up around the plants as they grow.

COLES, the word that describes the vegetable family including cabbage, Brussels sprouts, cauliflower, broccoli, kale, and kohlrabi, indicates one of the easiest groups of vegetables to know when to plant. When seedlings go on sale in the store, get them into the ground.

Basically, the entire family has an aversion to hot sun. The milder West Coast summers are no threat to the coles, but in areas with hotter summers they should be planted in August or September so the plants reach maturity in cool weather.

Cabbages are adapted to a wide variety of soils, but they are heavy feeders and require moisture and good fertile soil to produce properly. Be liberal in your applications of well-rotted manure and commercial fertilizer when the plants are put in. Add a top dressing of nitrate of soda once or twice while they grow.

Plant early cabbage varieties as soon as the ground is warm

Cabbage is the best-known of the cole group

enough to be worked. Put them a foot apart in rows that are about 2 feet apart. Late cabbages go in rows 3 feet apart with the plants spaced approximately 2 feet apart.

As with cabbages, you should mound up the ground around Brussels sprouts as they grow. This supports the heads. These small members of the cabbage family are a little hardier than their cousins and can be planted earlier than the rest of the cabbages. In mild climates, as in many parts of California, they can survive the winters with little difficulty. Plant the sprouts anytime in the spring up to June in rows about 3 feet apart.

You will find they do their best in a light, moist soil and should be cultivated freely.

One real challenge to the gardener can be raising a good crop of cauliflower. This sensitive vegetable must have cool weather to survive. It is also sensitive to low humidity, doing its best in damp conditions.

Plant early cauliflower a month or so before the last expected frost. For a fall crop, put the plants in when it is likely there will be no more hot weather. Space them 18 inches to 2 feet apart in rows at least 2 feet apart.

Like a lot of vegetables, cauliflower does best in a well-drained but moist and fertile soil. Try to keep the soil light acid, a pH of about 6.5. When the plants go in, make sure the soil has plenty of humus and give the area around each plant a shot of good commercial fertilizer.

Cauliflower is one of the few vegetables you should cultivate and treat one plant at a time. During the growth period, side-dress each plant with a spoonful of nitrate of soda 3 weeks after starting and then twice more, with 2 or 3 weeks between treatments. If the garden begins to dry out, or has been established in a dry area, it is good to sprinkle cauliflower with water daily.

When the cauliflower's curd, the white center, begins to appear, tie the heavy green outer leaves across it to protect it from the sun. Thus blanched, it will be white when harvested and not sunburnt.

Broccoli is grown like cabbage, but with a little extra care it can be grown in hotter weather.

Leafy kale is a very cold-hardy plant that often lives through northern winters. The plant is also resistant to heat but will get tough the hotter and dryer it becomes.

Plant kale in the late summer or fall by broadcasting the seeds and raking them into the ground. If you are planting kale in the spring, put it in rows about 2 feet apart. However you prefer to do it, thin to 8 inches to a foot apart after the plants begin to grow.

To get a good crop of kohlrabi, proceed as you would with cabbage. Put the plants approximately an inch apart and cover with less than an inch of soil. Thin the plants when they are 4 inches tall. Rows should be 15 to 18 inches apart, with the plants kept thinned to 2 or 3 inches apart. Kohlrabi, though a member of the cabbage family, is grown for its root, or rather stem, not its leaves.

For tenderness, you have to grow kohlrabi quickly. Cultivate shallow and add a top dressing to give it a boost once it is started.

POTATOES are not recommended as a vegetable for the small gardener to grow; they take a lot of room. But if you want to try, plant white potatoes in the early spring or midwinter in as well-drained and sandy a soil as you can find. The subsoil, however, should be capable of holding some moisture. Plant the potato eyes about 4 inches deep and 18 inches apart.

If you want yams or sweet potatoes, remember they are tropical vegetables. They are strictly for summer or for indoor growth in hot climates, and should be widely spaced in rich, sandy soil.

PERENNIALS include several vegetables considered delicacies by many food lovers. This select group includes asparagus, rhubarb, and artichokes. Shallots are a perennial, too, strictly speaking, but since the whole plant is pulled up when it is harvested, this quality of the plant of lasting more than a year is of little consequence.

For asparagus, the soil should be rich, sandy loam with a pH factor at or a little over 7. Asparagus does especially well in the delta area of the Sacramento and San Joaquin Rivers. Put asparagus sets into the ground in early spring, planting in a 12-inch-deep trench into the bottom of which about 6 inches of rotted manure has been worked. Water thoroughly. Make sure the sets reach no higher than 6 inches below the top of the trench. Cover them with about 2 inches of soil and water them well. As the plants grow, keep filling in the ditch but do not cover the crowns.

Rhubarb will do well in any well-drained soil that has been enriched with plenty of humus. It can also be sprouted indoors. Add approximately a half-cup of commercial fertilizer to the soil for each plant a week before planting. Put the roots about 2 inches deep and space them 4 or 5 feet apart with 5 feet between rows. Cultivate lightly to get rid of weeds and make sure the plants have ample water throughout the growing season.

Rhubarb, grown for its stems, is a perennial vegetable

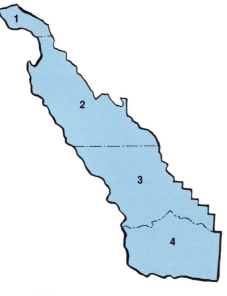

Artichokes come from California's four central coast counties

1. Santa Cruz

2. Monterey

3. San Luis Obispo

4. Santa Barbara

Although rhubarb is cold-hardy, it may die during the winter in cold climates. In warmer areas, it never stops growing.

Artichokes are a cool weather vegetable ideally suited to California's four central coastal counties (Santa Cruz, Monterey, San Luis Obispo, and Santa Barbara). Plant them in spring or fall 6 inches deep and about 4 feet apart with 4 feet between rows. You will need deep, fertile soil that is well drained and moisture-retentive. If necessary, install drainage ditches to be sure the plants do not stand in water.

Water your newly set plants thoroughly and see to it that the ground does not dry out after that. An injection of nitrogen fertilizer through the water every month is the normal practice with California artichoke growers. If you cannot do this, side-dress the plants in the spring when growth starts, using a half-cup of ammonium nitrate. Keep artichokes weeded and mulched with organic material.

EDIBLE LEAVES, of all the vegetable groups available to you, probably offer the broadest challenges, from simple to extremely difficult.

Spinach is a tough plant that needs slightly cool weather to grow. Sow the seeds in the spring as soon as the soil can be cultivated. If you start early enough, you can get two plantings in a single season.

Many varieties of lettuce can be grown in the home garden

For a fall spinach crop, sow a month or two before the first frost. In areas with cool climates, you can grow it continuously from spring to winter. If your area has mild winters, spinach can be an all-year crop.

Sow spinach seeds 2 to the inch and thin to 4 or 5 inches between plants when they are full-sized. Space rows at least a foot apart. Soil for spinach should be well drained, moisture-retentive, and filled with humus. Since spinach needs a nearly neutral pH, it is a good idea to mix about 8 ounces of a good, balanced fertilizer with the soil for every 50 feet of row.

Swiss chard is grown a lot like beets. Once the plants are in the ground, after the last hard frost, just get out of the way. Put chard in rows about a foot apart with the plants spaced 4 inches apart. When they start to crowd, thin them to 8 inches between and eat the ones you take out.

There are four basic types of lettuce: crisphead or heading; butterhead; leaf, bunching, loose-leafed, or loosehead; and romaine. Typical examples of each, in the order named, are Iceberg, Bibb, Ruby, Cos. Lettuce is a cool-weather crop and should be grown in the spring. In warmer climates, you can grow crisphead as a winter crop.

If seeds are used to start the crop, the seedlings should be moved to the garden about the time of the last freeze. Loose-leafed, butterhead, and some of the other hardier lettuces are usually grown by seeding the ground as soon as it is warm enough to be worked. It is possible to repeat the seeding once or twice at 3-week intervals to get a continuous lettuce supply.

For fall crops, plant early enough for the lettuce to mature just before the first hard frost. When you put in the seeds, place them a couple of inches apart. Thin crisphead to a foot between sets, butterheads to 7 or 8 inches, and leaf to 6 inches. There should be a foot between rows.

If you are going to get good lettuce, you have to start with good soil containing lots of humus. Add about 6 ounces of a balanced fertilizer for about 50 feet of row. Side-dress when the plants are about half grown and keep weeds out of the plot.

CELERY offers a real challenge. You will not find anything tougher than getting a good crop of celery. Buy sets at your nursery, start seeds in the house in the late winter or early spring, or plant seeds in the garden a few days before the last expected frost. If you start seeds in the house or in a cold frame, transplant when they are 2 to 4 inches tall. For a late crop you can sow the seeds in beds about 4 months before the first freeze.

Fumigate celery soil if there is any risk of nematodes. The soil must be well drained, moisture-retentive, fertile, and somewhat acid, with a pH of about 6.5. Give the ground a strong application of well-rotted manure or an application of peat, leaf mold, or other organic material. Add about 12 ounces of commercial fertilizer for every 50 square feet of ground. If the ground is short of boron, put on an ounce for the same area. Your ground must be well-crumbled, and it is a good idea to apply a fertilizer booster when sets are put in the ground. The sandier, more silty loam you have, the better your chances for celery, which prefers moist lowland to upland soil.

Plants should be put in about 6 inches apart in rows about a foot apart. If you use seeds, keep the bed covered with burlap or plastic sheets until they germinate. Make sure the ground stays moist.

Hopefully, your plants will not be in an area noted for bright,

Celery stalks can be used in everything from soups to salads or as a munching snack

sunny days. If they are, try to give them some shade. At the very least, attempt to plant the sets in cloudy weather. A balanced fertilizer side-dressing should be applied about a month after planting and a second time 2 months after the plants are in the ground. Keep them well watered, and cultivate shallowly but continuously to suppress weeds and keep the soil loose.

If you prefer white celery stalks to green, blanch the plants either by hilling earth against the growing stalks or by covering them with paper or some other opaque material. Do not cover the leaves, only the stalks.

All this may sound simple, but celery is a plant that will not tolerate extremely high or low temperature variations. It is a heavy consumer of water and nutrients.

OKRA should be put into well-prepared enriched soil when the ground has warmed and all risk of frost has passed. Put the plants about 8 inches apart in rows 2 to 3 feet apart. The soil must be acid, with a pH of 6 or less. Add a good supply of humus and about 8 ounces of fertilizer to every 50 feet of row.

Okra, sometimes over-
looked, is a useful veg-
etable, especially good
in soups

Okra will do well in hot, dry climates, but it does better if it is well watered. If you add side-dressing of nitrate of soda or a balanced fertilizer when the fruit begins to set and when growth starts to slow, it will help. Cultivate okra lightly to keep out the weeds.

TOMATOES can produce under a great variety of conditions, but they like full sun best. Put them into well-prepared soil, conditioned with an earlier application of manure or fertilizer. Try to keep the nitrogen level down. Although it aids plant (leaf) growth, excess nitrogen could halt the development of fruit.

Since tomatoes are undoubtedly the most popular of all plants for the home gardener, varieties have been developed for every kind of growing condition, as well as many different varieties destined for such purposes as eating in salads or for cooking. There are early and late tomatoes suited to cool temperatures, and there are hot-weather tomatoes less temperamental about really high heat. The ''beef'' tomatoes with much solid flesh contrast with juicy tomatoes with more plentiful seed. The very popular small-fruit tomatoes include cherry tomatoes, plum tomatoes, and pear tomatoes. Obtain guidance about which varieties are suited to your plot and purpose from your nurseryman or county agent, though, briefly, such varieties as Ace and Pearson are good mid-season producers and Small Fry is a superlative miniature tomato.

58

Tomatoes are best bought as seedlings in flats, but they may be started from seed indoors about 6 weeks before the last expected frost. Some plants may even be maintained as house pets, grown in pots or other containers the year round. Growing the smaller varieties this way may prove to be especially gratifying. Perhaps the best approach is to try two or three plants each of a number of varieties and sizes. It is sometimes literally amazing how much fruit one 6-foot tomato plant can produce.

Plant tomatoes after all risk of frost has passed, but do not wait too long. Some tomatoes have a habit of shedding their blossoms in summer when the temperature goes over 90. In areas that have long summers, you may be able to get two crops by planting in the spring and again in the early fall.

Although good sun is needed for these plants, try to protect them from hot, dry winds. That, too, may retard fruit growth.

When you put in your sets, plant them deep—about two-thirds of the plant—in the ground. Water the new sets thoroughly and add a cup of commercial starter solution to each plant. You can get good results by putting some manure into the holes when plants are set. If you do, make the hole deeper and put the manure at the bottom. Cover it with about 4 inches of soil and then put in the plants.

Tomatoes, the mainstay of the home gardener, come in a variety of sizes for a myriad of uses

Space staked tomatoes approximately 2 or 3 feet apart, and in rows from 3 to 5 feet apart, depending on the varieties you are growing. Make sure they get plenty of water until just before harvesting begins, but do not flood them to the point that the fruit cracks.

Fertilize the plants lightly with a side-dressing of balanced fertilizer at a month and two months after they are in the ground. Don't overfeed or underfeed; just make sure that the plants get the nitrogen they need when the fruit begins to grow.

As earlier mentioned, tomatoes may lose their blooms if they are too young when hit by hot weather. On the other hand, they will also lose blossoms in areas where nighttime temperatures drop below 55 degrees. Talk to your county agent or garden shop operator about adding a plant hormone that will stop or at least minimize this.

You can ride the magic carpet of a tremendous variety of vegetables, ranging from the commonplace to quite exotic plants, in your most creative flights of fancy. The adaptations available for disease resistance, weather, or soil variations in your area are almost infinite. And the different conditions each one needs to produce well are just as variable.

Sometimes a couple of city blocks can make a world of difference between your garden and that of a friend. For your particular garden to succeed, or for a particular vegetable to succeed in your garden, you will need very specific information, and you should feel free to tap every resource you can find. Local agricultural schools, county agents, extension services, and garden shop operators, as well as more experienced gardeners nearby, are all good sources and should be used to their fullest. Experience, too, is a great teacher. If you'd like to grow something in your garden, try. Failure, if you do fail, may be instructive and some variation of the pattern next year or next growing season may well succeed. The important thing is to watch carefully and intelligently—the experts may well be wrong about your specific situation.

5 Herbs

Probably the most widely grown plants in the world are herbs. You can find them growing in gardens, in window boxes, and even in flower pots, in all sorts of climates and soils.

Maybe it is because they often look delicate, or possibly because they are used so sparingly and contribute such delicate tastes and aromas to our food, but many gardeners seem to be afraid of trying to grow herbs. They react as if you had suggested they try growing orchids in Alaska. Don't get caught in that trap. A lot of herbs are tough. They can survive in terrains and climates that will stop trees cold. You can find herbs growing in the European Alps well above timber line in rocky ground and biting cold where only they, and a few mosses, survive.

All through recorded history, man has grown or searched the woodlands for these fragrant plants—for their magical-mystical properties, as medicinal potions and mixtures, or for the added zest they give his food.

Today, some herbs are still used as medicines, but perfectly healthy gardeners cultivate many more than medicinal herbs simply to spice up otherwise bland food.

But before the first herb goes into the ground, you have planning to do. There are all sorts of possible arrangements for herbs in your garden. You can put them in an out-of-the-way corner, along an ugly fence as decoration, or in patterns that break up or enhance the arrangement of vegetable rows and hills.

Your main considerations in organizing herb beds are available sunlight, the presence of shade, and how easily you can get to the plants once they are growing. Most herbs are sun-lovers, but some require shade now and then. Also, since there is a wide variation in the height to which various herbs grow, you may find that you have screened yourself from the shorter plants if you put the taller herbs in front.

Fortunately, herbs are a forgiving sort of greenery. They thrive in well-drained, light soils. But marjoram, thyme, and some others will do well if you ground is alkaline; and angelica, bergamot, chamomile, chervil, and the mints often do better when your ground is a little heavy, somewhat more clayey than normal. You can find wild herbs growing among the rocks on what appears to be an almost soilless stone crag.

If your soil is heavy clay, you can expect your major difficulties in periods when it is too wet to be worked. Cuttings will not root well in wet clay, and seed beds are a constant source of irritation because you cannot work them. Add peat, straw, compost, and other humus-producing organic matter to the topsoil to loosen up the clay for herbs just as you did for your vegetables.

If you have light, sandy soil, you have ideal ground for herbs that had their origin in the warm weather of southern Europe, such as rosemary and sage. Chalky soils are good, too, but they may cause your herb blossoms to change color. It is a good idea to have your soil tested before you start growing herbs, especially if there is any chance that you may have a lime deficiency. You may want to add lime to the herb plot each year since the weather is always leaching the mineral out of the ground, and herbs require a lot of it.

About the only thing most herbs (or most plants, for that matter) will not tolerate is waterlogged roots. Your soil must have good drainage. But even if your garden sometimes looks like the

Herbs are easily planted in the garden from seedlings available in plant stores or from plant racks

second cousin of a swamp with water standing all over it, you will find that broom and foxglove love it.

Don't worry too much about the weather; it has to be pretty extreme to harm most herbs. As a rule, however, guard them from wind and frost.

If you plant the biennial and perennial herbs, you can be pretty sure they will survive miserably damp winters and come on strong again the next year. But in areas of really severe cold, you will have to grow the more tender ones like annuals to get any worthwhile production.

As a rule herbs are good drought resisters, even in the hottest climates. This is fortunate because watering an herb patch of any size will do bad things to a water bill in a hurry. To water a patch of most herbs properly, you would have to play the hose on it for about twenty minutes to reach the deep soil layers around the longer herb roots. If you do try watering, it cannot be skimpy if it is to do any good for most herbs. If you only wet the surface of the ground and do not reach the deep soil layers, as with all plants, the roots of the herbs will begin to grow up to reach the moisture. And once you start a watering program, the herbs will get used to it fast. Unless you want them to have serious trouble, you'll have to continue watering— want to or not—until the next good rain.

For annuals and herbs that you treat like annuals, plant in the spring—April or early May. Sow them in furrows or drills about 8 inches apart. When the seedlings are large enough to handle, thin them to about 3 inches between plants. As they grow, you can thin the plants to anything from 6 inches to a 3 foot spacing depending on how big you expect them to get.

Another planting method is to broadcast the seeds over an area and rake them into the soil. Thin them in two stages as they grow.

Cultivation of herbs is much like the cultivation of other plants. They need to be hoed and weeded until they get a good start. Once they get started, herbs will usually proliferate so well that weeds will have no chance against them. Keep the top layer of soil in the herb bed loose to retain moisture.

Most herbs are not heavy feeders. If you do use chemical plant foods, be careful not to overfeed the plants; you can do more harm than good. If you use manure, it should be dug into the soil before planting. You may want to fork in a light application of compost after the plants get started, but this treatment is not essential.

In areas with extremely cold winters or hot summers, mulch around the plants to keep in the heat or moisture.

Although we are concentrating here on herbs for use as edible plants, don't overlook the ornamental value these plants have. Their leafage and flowers can add spots of beauty to your kitchen garden; their fine odors add another sensory dimension to gardening. Do not forget, either, that formal arrangements are possible with these plants, which take very well to being trimmed and clipped like a hedge.

Among the many garden herbs of the world, several can be used in cooking. Let us take a quick look at a couple of dozen—and more— to see how they are used and what you have to do to get them to grow.

Anise

ANISE. Plant this 2-foot-tall, graceful annual with one foot spacing between plants. Place it in well-drained loam where it can get full sun, and thin the plants out as you think necessary. Anise's green leaves are used in soups, salads, stews, and as a garnish. The seeds can be used in cakes and cookies.

ANGELICA. Sow the seeds of this 6-foot biennial herb thickly. Start it in the early spring before the last frost or in the late fall. When the plants come up, thin to a couple of feet between plants. Angelica should be placed in rich, humus-filled soil with a handful of balanced fertilizer raked into the bed. Make sure the plant is in the sun, but give it some daily shade if possible. The hollow stem of this plant is candied and eaten as a confection. Parts of the stem can also be cooked with rhubarb or rhubarb jam to remove tartness.

Lemon Balm

BALM. A member of the mint family, balm should be seeded about an eighth of an inch deep, a foot between plants, in average or better garden soil. This foot-high perennial can make do in either the sun or light shade with a little fertilizer added to the soil. The leaves are a garnish for summer coolers; you also might like them in salads. Use them either fresh or dried and ground in fish sauces, in stuffing, or as a lemon substitute. In fact, the variety generally grown is called lemon balm.

Sweet Basil

BASIL. Another member of the mint family, basil should be planted outdoors after all risk of frost is passed. Put it in a sunny spot, in ordinary garden soil. Place the seeds a quarter of an inch deep, thin the plants to about a foot apart, and space the rows the same distance. Both sweet basil and bush basil are commonly grown, but sweet basil is ordinarily used as a flavoring. This 2-foot high, clove-scented, annual herb is a favorite to flavor tomato and mock turtle soups, tomato dishes, salads, omelets, chopped meats of all sorts, and especially sausage.

Borage

BORAGE. Sow this herb at the last spring freeze, and thin to a couple of feet between plants when they come up. This annual can be put in poor, rocky, or sandy soil and it will produce bushy plants 2 or 3 feet tall where few other plants could hope to survive. The seeds should go in about an eighth of an inch deep along with a little fertilizer. Weeding, and some watering in very dry weather, is all you need to do. You can candy the small blue flowers of this herb and use the cucumber-flavored leaves fresh as a garnish for drinks, as a parsley-like garnish, or dried and ground as the base for a tea.

BURNET. An 18-inch perennial herb, this plant produces young leaves you can eat. Their cucumber-like flavor is good in salads or as a garnish in cool drinks. Sow the seeds about as you would borage. Burnet will grow in practically any soil as long as it has full sun. Space the plants about a foot apart in rows a foot apart, and leave the fertilizer and water for other plants; this one doesn't need them.

CARAWAY. A 2-foot biennial, caraway is a plant you can grow in either light shade or bright sun. The seeds should be sown as soon as the ground can be worked in the spring; mix in humus and a balanced fertilizer. Dig the soil deep for a caraway bed, and keep it well watered. The next spring add a side-dressing of fertilizer. In addition to using the seeds in all kinds of baked goods (typically this is the familiar curved seed used in rye breads), salads, and cream cheeses, as well as an after-dinner stomach-settler, you can use the leaves of the plant in salads, stews, and soups.

CATNIP. This should be planted about the end of June. Put it in the sun or partial shade. Average soil will do well enough as long as you add a little commercial fertilizer. The plants and rows should be a little over a foot apart. Use the minty leaves of this 3-foot perennial either green or dried as seasoning or as a tea base. Of course, if you live with a cat, this is its special treat.

CHERVIL. An annual, chervil can be planted any time from spring to fall in a series of sowings. Thin the plants to about 6 inches apart after they start, and add a little water in dry weather. Chervil gets to be about 12 to 15 inches high. The leaves, chopped fresh, make a good flavoring for salads, tartar sauce, or soups. Dried, you can add them to stuffings. You can also use chervil in making vinegar for salad dressings.

CHIVES. Plant about a foot apart in the spring. The tops of this perennial herb, cut regularly, will give you a mild oniony flavoring for salads and egg or cheese dishes. It is also good in tartar sauce. This

Chives

is one of those herbs whose flowers, lavender pompons, make a most attractive display in garden borders. The plant itself is somewhat less than a foot tall and should be kept picked of its flowers if it is flavorful stems you want.

70

Coriander

CORIANDER. A tough annual herb, coriander grows to a height of about 2 feet. Sow the seeds at monthly intervals throughout the spring and fall, thinning the seedlings to about a foot apart as they grow. Average soil is sufficient for coriander as long as you spade it deep and add a little fertilizer. Put the seeds about an eighth of an inch deep. Coriander seeds taste a little like orange rind and can be used in baked foods or salad dressings.

CUMIN. Sow this 6-inch annual herb after the last frosty day in spring. The plants should be about a foot apart, in rows about 6 to 8 inches apart. Feed the plants at least once during the season and see that they have water. The seeds are used in pickles and curries for flavor.

Dill   **Fennel**

DILL. Sow after all danger of frost is gone. Dill, a 3-foot annual, does best if you put it in a sunny spot protected from the wind. Give it a little fertilizer; however, the ground doesn't need to be better than average. Once the plants are growing, thin them to a 6-inch spacing in rows about a foot apart. Both dill weed (the leaves or stems) and seed are used by the cook. Dill leaves and shoots flavor fish sauces, potato salad, and cottage cheese dishes. Dried, you can use dill leaf in stews, soups or omelets. Use the seeds for pickling, in vinegar, or for making condiments.

FENNEL. Sweet fennel is a perennial, growing 4 or 5 feet tall. Plant in well-prepared, rich soil in the early spring. Thin the stand to about 10 inches between plants. Use the leaves either fresh or dried for tea or in sauces. The licorice-flavored seeds can be sprinkled in soup or pastry fillngs. Cooked, the thick stalks are much like celery or shredded fresh into a salad. Florence fennel, or finocchio, is a close relative, used cooked or raw like celery which it resembles physically in its overlapping stalks. But it is finocchio's stalks, not its leaves or seeds, that are used, especially in Italian cookery. This variety is an annual, growing to only about 2 feet in height.

Horehound

HOREHOUND. A 2-foot perennial, horehound is traditionally used to make candy or as a tea to ward off colds. Put the seeds in the ground an eighth of an inch deep in rows, and thin to a foot between plants. Plant horehound in the sun in average soil containing a little humus. Add a little fertilizer side-dressing each spring.

LOVAGE. A perennial, lovage can be sown in late spring or early fall. The plants should be transplanted the next summer in well-drained, humus-filled soil. Space the plants a couple of feet apart in rows with the same separation. Side-dress with fertilizer every spring and water during very dry periods. Put lovage in a spot with full sun for the best results; however, it can produce in light shade. This plant can grow to anywhere between 3 and 6 feet in height. The leaves have a celery/parsley flavor and you can use them either dry or fresh for seasoning.

73

Marjoram　　　　　　　　　　　　**Pineapple Mint**

MARJORAM. This perennial (in California) does best in hot, dry places, with plants spaced about a foot apart. Leave them alone unless they refuse to grow or start looking sick. They should be bushy and between 9 and 12 inches high. This herb's leaves are used in soups, egg dishes, dressings, and vinegars. They also make a good addition to meat, tomato, and mushroom dishes.

MINT. Plant this hardy perennial in fertile soil. The soil can have a heavy clay content, as all mint really needs to thrive is plenty of moisture. You can grow it in either the sun or partial shade, and it needs weeding only until it spreads and takes over the patch. Thin the bed every two or three years to a space of about a foot between plants. These 18-inch plants will invade every part of your garden unless they are kept under control. Plastic or metal strips around the bed will keep the runners in their place. There are many recognizable flavors: spearmint, peppermint (described separately in this chapter), orange mint, apple or round-leaved mint, are those principally grown. You can enjoy mint in sauces, jellies, butter, or tea; it is, of course, the most noted garnish or jelly used with lamb. And you can use a sprig on iced drinks or cook its leaves with vegetables.

Oregano

NASTURTIUM. An annual that grows in poor soil, the nasturtium is commonly a climber, or it may be a smaller plant about a foot high. Plants should be spaced about 6 inches apart, and take little cultivation. The leaves and flowers are used to season salads, while the seeds are a good substitute for capers.

OREGANO. Planted about the time of the last frost, oregano is later transplanted into stands with about 18 inches between plants and rows. Just press the seeds gently into ground that will get full sunlight. Given an average soil with a little humus, you can expect a good crop from this 2-foot perennial. It should be fertilized once a year with a balanced plant food. Fresh or dried, use the leaves as seasoning.

Parsley

PARSLEY. A cold-hardy biennial, parsley can be grown as an annual. The leaves are springier and tastier when the plant is treated as an annual. Transplant it from flats into the garden about the time of the last freeze. In warm areas, you can also plant in late summer or fall. The plants should be about 6 inches apart in rows a foot between. Parsley will do well in sun or shade as long as the soil is moist. It needs only average soil, incidentally. In warmer areas, your plants will last through the winter if you give them protection, and they will make new growth the second year. Parsley will grow up to 3 feet high; the leaves are cut for use when they are about 6 inches long. Depending on which variety you have grown, parsley can be used as a flavoring or a garnish.

PEPPERMINT. Plant in the early spring in moist, sandy ground. This perennial is vigorous in warm, wet areas, growing to a height of nearly 2 feet. Put the plants about 9 inches apart. Fresh or dried peppermint leaves are used in teas, jellies, beverages, and other sweets.

Rosemary

ROSE GERANIUM. A very delicate perennial, the rose geranium has perfumed leaves that are used as a garnish or for flavor in apple jelly. Grow it in pots filled with a mix of one part peat, one part sand, and three parts loam, with a small amount of bonemeal. As the plants get bigger (as a pot plant it will get to be 2 feet tall), transplant them into larger pots. Keep them indoors when there is a threat of chill. This is an especially good herb for indoor gardening. In mild areas, where frost is not killing, this herb can be grown outside the year round. In the ground, it grows to 4 or more feet high.

ROSEMARY. Leaves of this tradition-filled herb add flavor to soups, stews, meat dishes, and sauces. Grow rosemary in full sun in ground that has a pH of about 7 (neutral). Plant it about the end of June, and mix a little fertilizer with the soil. Side-dress this perennial with fertilizer each spring. Individual plants should be about 3 feet apart with the same spacing between the rows. Given the right conditions, rosemary will get to be 6 feet high, though usually it is somewhat smaller.

Sage

SAGE. Bushes should be planted in light, well-drained soil between the last frost and the first of June. Mix some fertilizer with the soil and put the plants and rows about 2 feet apart. Side-dress every spring to keep this aromatic 2-foot perennial going. Its leaves will season fish, meats, poultry, stews, and dressings. Garden sage, incidentally, is a Salvia, related to the red-flowered plant seen in flower gardens; it is not the sagebrush of Western deserts, which is an artemisia, of bitter taste and a close cousin to tarragon.

Summer savory

SUMMER SAVORY. Plant this 18-inch annual in well-prepared, fairly rich soil after the last frost. The plants should be about 6 inches apart, with about a foot between rows. Add about a cup of balanced fertilizer to every 30 feet of row, and water the plants when the weather is dry. The leaves make a flavoring for vegetables, salads, gravies, dressings, soups, sausages, meats, or poultry, or they can be used as a garnish.

TARRAGON. This aromatic herb is used for vinegar and as a seasoning for a wide variety of dishes. Plant it in fairly dry ground, where it will get full sun. The plants should be about 2 feet apart with the same spacing for rows. This 18-inch perennial can be watered in especially dry spells, but if you give it too much water, tarragon will rot.

79

Thyme

THYME. A perennial, thyme should be planted in early spring. It grows to a height of about a foot. Keep the soil well drained and limed with a little fertilizer. Side-dress it every spring and try to keep the ground moist until the young plants have gotten a good start. Space the plants about 8 inches apart, with a foot or more between rows. Thyme adds flavor to stuffings for veal, fish, poultry, stews, or casseroles.

WINTER SAVORY. Used like summer savory, this foot-high perennial herb can be planted in poor soil as long as it has plenty of sun and lime. Planting can be done in the spring or early fall; plants should be side-dressed with a balanced fertilizer each spring.

6 Herb Culture

Herbs usually do their best in light, open soil of moderate fertility as long as they have good drainage.

Prepare your ground normally, getting rid of the weeds and working in sand, peat, or other material that will open up the soil if it is heavy. Keep in mind that most herbs like well-limed ground, and since the mineral is constantly being lost by weathering it is a good idea to lime your herb ground every year.

Many herbs first developed in southern Europe and the world's other areas of warm climate. Thus, most herbs thrive in warm, sunny weather. But here, too, you will find herbs that do well in partial shade—alexanders, angelica, chervil, chives, sweet cicely, ferns, lovage, meadowsweet, parsley, poke root, valerian, and woodruff. This shade, however, should be no heavier than what you would find in an open forest. Deep, long-term shading can have a detrimental effect on your herbs.

Quite apart from their use as food is the decorative quality of herbs. The herb grower often needs no other excuse for giving space to one of these appealing plants. You can grow them in a border hedge or in irregular patches that break up the straight rows or ordered hills of your vegetable garden. You can grow herbs of varying heights close to each other without shading out the short ones. Herbs will even grow in dirt-filled chinks in rock walls. If you plan to use your herbs for decoration as well as for the kitchen, be sure you relate the amount of herbs you plant to the amount you can use. Herbs grow—and many of them spread—rapidly. If there are too many for your use, they will soon start looking untidy and will detract more than they add to your garden's appearance.

Another good use for herbs, especially if your plot is on sloping ground, is as a soil binder. Borage, a relatively tall herb at 3 feet, prostrate rosemary, which reaches approximately 15 inches, and silver or lemon thyme, 6 inches high, are all drought-resistant herbs that spread quickly and will help keep soil from washing away.

Herbs are especially good for the urban indoor garden. With care, they will thrive in window boxes, wooden tubs, clay pots, or almost any container you can devise. All you have to do is make sure the plants get the light they need. If the herbs you are growing are varieties that do well with some shade or in a cool spot, try to put them where they will have these conditions. If, on the other hand, you are growing sun-worshippers and they must get their light through a glass window, don't forget that glass-filtered light creates drought conditions. Take care to keep these plants moist.

If possible, try to adapt your heating system to your indoor plants, or your plants to your heating. Plants with thick leaves often suffer in dry heat, while others may do best in oil-stove heating. The only way to be sure about which herbs will grow best in your home is trial and error. If you want to add moisture to the air, one way is to evaporate water from a bowl on or near your heater. You may need to spray the leaves of some plants with water and wash the dust off periodically.

It is essential that your indoor herbs get the water they need, but also you must make sure that they are properly drained. If they sit in excessively damp soil, herbs will die faster than they would from too little watering. From early winter until March or April, herbs need no more than one or two tablespoons of water every week to ten days. Plants that lose their leaves and go dormant during this period can be set aside in a relatively cool spot.

An indoor herb garden. Seedlings should be quickly transplanted to larger containers once they reach this size

Probably the most important factor in growing herbs indoors is providing them with soil deep enough for their roots. The 2- or 3-inch-deep planters you can buy almost anywhere may fit nicely into your home decor; but before you buy them imagine how your home will look with dead herbs, then buy the deepest planters you can find.

There is little reason to water hardy herbs growing outdoors unless you live in an arid region or are suffering a severe drought. If watering becomes necessary, be sure to do a thorough job. Soak the ground well enough to make sure the water reaches 18 inches to 2 feet deep, down where the roots are, and keep it up until the next good rain.

If you feel the need to fertilize your herb beds, you'll be safe using either organic or synthetic plant foods. You can make the synthetic type last longer if you get the kind composed of rock-hard granules that dissolve and release their nutrients slowly. Overfeeding with quick-dissolving fertilizer can cause osmosis in the wrong direction—the concentration of plant food in the soil will draw water from the plant instead of the plant drawing water from the soil.

As with vegetables in the garden, your herb patch will benefit from the wind protection provided by a fence

Manures and composts are generally slower acting than synthetic fertilizers. You can get the best results from them, and save some of your summer time, by applying them in the winter.

To get the utmost from your plants, feed them once when they show their first growth of the year and again in late June or when you make your first cuttings. Try to fertilize in rainy weather. The nutrients get into the ground sooner and protect the plants from being "burned" by heavy concentrations.

One main concern for your herbs should be protection from the wind. A solid fence or a row of trees or shrubs will protect them adequately. To enhance protection from the winds, consider planting the taller varieties closest to your fence or hedge. This barrier will filter and limit the air coming through and force the rest of it up and away from your plants. By the time the flowing air descends, it will be beyond the tall, fragile plants. As with vegetables, it is necessary to avoid planting herbs in frost pockets.

Your herb patch need not be laid out in rows; plant them as decorative enhancement to the yard

After your herbs get started, you will seldom have to weed the patch. Many herbs spread very quickly and dominate their surroundings. Once thus established, they will take care of the weeds.

Plant diseases and insects are seldom a problem with herbs. Some herbs are open to rust or mold attack, and mint may suffer from fungus, but successful disease assaults on herbs are usually indications of poor feeding and can be corrected by improving the ground's fertility and removing the infected plants.

Annual herbs and those that cannot survive their winter surroundings are usually propagated by seed sown fresh in April, early May, or whenever the ground is warm enough. When possible, and when you have plants designed to thrive under your particular conditions, however, you should propagate in ways that will insure continuation of the healthy stock. Many herbs—sage, thyme, and savory among them—are "stem rooters." Wherever their stems touch the ground, small clumps of roots begin to form. You can encourage this habit by burying much of the old plant in the fall so that only the newest leafy shoots are in the open. Dig it out in the spring and you should be able to cut off all the new plants you can use. Mints and other plants that send out runners form roots at their joints. It should be easy for you to detach them from their parent and plant them.

Some perennial herbs, as we noted earlier, can be propagated by merely pulling them up and dividing the roots, while lavender, rosemary, southernwood, cotton lavender, and others can be propagated by planting cuttings.

Most planting of anything besides seeds should be done in the fall until the end of November, or in the early spring from February to May. In areas of severe winters or heavy cold ground—like some of the California coastal areas—it is safest to plant in the spring. If you would like to plant cuttings in the fall, it is less risky to use a cold frame. Make sure the cuttings, which should be about 4 inches long, are planted with half their length in the ground and are kept tightly packed.

However you start them, be sure your herbs have plenty of room when they are set in their permanent locations. Lavender sets should have 4 to 6 feet around them, rosemary at least 3, and sage, savory, and thyme at least a foot between plants and double that between rows.

We've said nothing in this book about vegetable harvesting

Drying herbs in a well-aired, shaded spot

because most of them are annuals and the proper methods of harvesting are obvious: you pull up a radish, carrot, or turnip; you cut lettuce and cabbage; you pick off tomatoes, peppers, squash. Herbs, however, are another matter and must be harvested properly to retain their value. You should know which part of the plant to use and how to get it.

Be sure you harvest herbs when they are dry. Avoid harvesting in rainy weather and wait late enough in the day for the morning dew to dry. Gather your herbs in a relatively flat container and avoid crushing or bruising them. Since they do not retain their strength for long periods, you should gather only the amount you can use in a reasonably short time.

To harvest herb roots, take up the mature plants, wash the roots clean, and drain off all water. Trim away any tough, fibrous material and all underground stems.

Clip flowers the day before they mature to retain their oils. And since only perfect blooms will not deteriorate during the drying process, they should be insect-free. They should be washed clean as soon as they are cut.

Leaves, too, should be cut when the plant is most alive—just before it blooms. Take only leaves free of insect or disease damage.

If you want to use the whole plant, pull it up while it is in bloom and wash it clean. To get only that part of the plant above ground, cut it off *after* it has flowered.

Dry your herbs indoors in a shaded spot with good ventilation. But roots should be dried in total sun. To start the process, try to keep the temperature at a steady 90 degrees. Avoid any area with high humidity, such as a kitchen, bathroom, laundry room, or basement. As soon as you have your harvest, spread the plants in a shallow, open container, on cheesecloth or wire mesh. Be sure that they don't touch or overlap each other and keep the different herbs separated. To conserve space, you can hang bunches of sage (salvia) and artemisia (wormwood or tarragon) upside down from the rafters of your drying room. Air should circulate easily around all drying herbs.

After the first twenty-four hours, you can lower the temperature of the drying room as long as it never falls below 72 degrees lest the plants absorb moisture and rot. Turn the herbs twice during the first twenty-four hours and then daily until they are dry. Don't try to rush the drying, as that can be as harmful as letting the herbs get damp. You will find that leaves and flowers are ready first, stems dry next, and roots are done last. When herbs are dry enough to break easily in your hand, they are ready.

As soon as they are dried, crumble the herbs in your hand, remove and discard twigs and unnecessary woody pieces, and store the herbs in airtight jars, bottles, boxes, or bins until you need them. They shouldn't be allowed to collect dust that will wind up in your food, and they will lose their qualities in the open air.

7 Artificial Environments

Essentially, anything you do to protect your plants from nature creates an artificial environment. It can be anything from a light application of mulch to keeping your plants indoors throughout their lives.

Mulching

Probably the simplest form of plant protection is mulching—spreading ground-up organic or inorganic material around and over the growing plants. Of all the defenses you can find, mulching is one of the most versatile and one of the simplest for you to use. It will keep your garden cool in blistering heat, help keep it warm on frosty nights, and hold in moisture against drying winds. A good application of mulch will even help suppress weeds.

Usually, a mulch should be applied after your plants are tall enough to stand above it. You should lay it close enough around the plants to give them the appearance of growing out of it instead of the ground. Be sure that the mulch does not pack down too tightly. A mulch of fine material such as grass cuttings should be mixed with twigs or other springy material to keep it loose and permit air to get into it.

If you mulch too deeply or pack it too tightly, you can be

threatening your vegetables and herbs. In wet climates, very heavy or tight mulching can keep the ground soggy and cut off your plants' air supply. In extremely dry areas, a heavy mulching can block the little available rain and soak it up before it reaches the ground and your plants' roots. The conditions described, of course, are directly related to the cool, damp coastal areas of California, as well as the arid regions of the interior Southwest.

You should also be aware of the pests prevalent in your area before picking a mulch or deciding whether to use one at all. Slugs, snails, earwigs, sow bugs (pill bugs), cutworms, centipedes, mice, and several kinds of beetle love to move into a well-prepared mulch bed. And you might not find clues left by gophers and moles until it is too late if they can go about their work under the cover of a mulch layer.

The best guide to when and how much to mulch in your area is experience. Until you have gained such experience, discuss the use of mulches in detail with your garden shop operator, your county agent, or experienced gardeners in your neighborhood.

Another consideration in using mulch is deciding the kind that is best suited for your purposes—organic or inorganic. If you decide on undecomposed vegetable matter—ground-up tree cuttings, hay, grass clippings, straw, peat, peanut hulls, leaves, cut-up weeds, or the like—you should be prepared for a nitrogen drop in your soil when the mulch begins to decompose. The microorganisms that break the mulch down use up the nitrogen and keep it from your plants. If you have soil overly rich in nitrogen, there is nothing to worry about. You can also alleviate the situation by adding a nitrogen-rich fertilizer to the plot.

Good inorganic mulches can be created from plastic and paper. (True, paper is organic, but years will be needed before it breaks down into usable soil elements, so we treat it as inorganic material.) You can buy polyethylene film in rolls for spreading between your plant rows. It comes either clear (to let in the sun) or black (to keep it out). Either way, the plastic helps keep in the heat and moisture and has a tendency to shade out weeds.

Problems with strips of mulching material. Preventing wind from tearing it up requires some ingenuity

Rolls of butcher paper, metal foil, or newspaper laid over the ground will do the same thing as the plastic and may be cheaper for your home garden. Metal foil will give you the added advantage of reflecting some additional light onto the leafage of your plants, an especially desirable plus factor in some of the coastal, cloudy areas where getting your plants enough sun can be a problem.

The main trouble with plastic, foil, or paper mulches is finding a way to keep them in place. If you do not somehow pin them down, the first breeze will pile them in a corner or scatter them all over the neighborhood.

Some truck farmers attach their mulch strips to stakes, but that requires a lot of cutting of holes or nailing. Another method you can use to secure paper, foil, or plastic is to pile dirt along its edges. Some gardeners go so far as to bury the whole thing in an effort to improve their garden's appearance.

However you do it, don't forget the pests. All you have to do is get your cover so securely in place that it is almost impossible to remove, and you will find a mole or gopher at work somewhere under it. The same situation will exist if you have to go after some plant diseases or insects hiding under the mulch.

Some gardeners have found that they can create the same effect as mulching by shallow cultivation. They say this creates a layer of dust "mulch." The problem is that this approach opens the way to extensive wind erosion if your garden is in a breezy area. And if the soil is clayey, the dust will probably cause puddling when it rains. In fact, if you decide on dust "mulching," be prepared to do the whole job of cultivating over again each time it rains.

For tall or climbing plants you can get some of the temperature protection that a mulch provides for smaller plants by wrapping the plants in cornstalks which are tied in place. You can achieve the same results by staking a cylinder of chicken wire around the plant and carefully stuffing the container with hay or straw.

As you have probably gathered, mulches are primarily a way of insulating your plants. It cannot keep them cool in extended hot spells or warm in biting cold, and it cannot keep your plants moist if there is no moisture available. If you must control extremes of temperature or moisture, you will have to create a more artificial environment than mulch offers.

Hot caps and frames

One of the simplest and most popular ways to protect your plants from cold is the hot cap and its variations. The hot cap is simply a tent of paraffin-treated paper or clear plastic film.

Placed over each one of your plants and secured with dirt or rocks, the translucent tent lets the sun in when it is shining and traps the heat radiating from the soil and the living plant when the weather is cold. Moisture evaporating from the soil and the plant forms droplets inside the hot cap that drip back to the ground.

Variations on the hot cap idea range from something as simple as putting cardboard boxes over the plants to windows built over the rows. If you cut the top of a box on three sides, leaving the fourth side attached as a hinge, it can be opened during the day to let in the sun and closed at night to hold in the heat. Try this with the bottoms of milk containers for smaller plants. Two window sashes can be connected with hinges and propped or hung from a frame over your

Frames and hot caps in various guises. A pair of hinged window frames or a carton opened top and bottom can be used to protect larger plants

plants like a tent to protect them from frost, also.

Between these extremes are an array of frames over which you stretch plastic sheeting and secure it to the ground. The variations usually depend on the size of the plants, the area you want to protect, and the materials on hand. Frames can be made from wood or from coat hangers, among other things.

If your problem is too much sun or wind, a good sheet of burlap or canvas is your best friend. A circle of wire set around your plant and draped with cloth to cover half the top and the side in the wind's direction is a simple and effective way of providing protection from both sun and wind. You can get wind protection by tacking the material to stakes upwind of your plants.

A good shade can also be built by constructing a lath screen above your plants. Build a frame out of 1x2 inch or heavier lumber, with at least one corner-to-corner support. The easiest way to space the lath is to cover the frame completely but nail down every other one; then remove the unnailed pieces. Be sure you nail onto the diagonal brace to stiffen the structure.

Once the shade is built, it can be laid over the plants on stake or brick supports or propped like a lean-to on stakes, depending on your needs.

Plastic, cheesecloth, or plywood tacked to frames and propped against a wall make easy shade and wind protection for seedling beds.

Mini-greenhouses

The use of cold frames and hot beds to start seeds was discussed earlier. Here are some details of their construction and how to use them as mini-greenhouses.

Basically, the cold frame is a slant-roofed wooden box with a transparent top. When the cold frame is built on the ground, the corner box supports are usually left long, sharpened into stakes, and driven into the ground. Earlier, we talked about how to build up the soil bed within the box.

The top of the cold frame need be nothing more than a sheet of plastic stapled into place on a removable frame. On more permanent installations, you may hinge window sash to the box walls. The angle of the slanted roof should be determined for your specific considerations. It should provide maximum sunlight exposure. If you need some shade build a lath shade that will fit over the glass top or will replace it in the summer. Also, try to provide some sort of propping to hold the frame lid open and let in air whenever possible.

As we have said, the only difference between a cold frame and a hot bed is the installation of a heating element. By far the best are heating cables made for hot beds. Laid in U-shaped loops about 3 inches from side to side not quite touching the ends of the box, they will keep the soil warm enough to encourage plant roots.

To construct a hot bed, you should put down a one-inch bed of sand, install the heating cable, add another inch-thick layer of sand, then a layer of inch wire mesh, and finally another inch of sand, before putting in the topsoil or soil substitute.

Now, take your cold frame or hot bed out of the garden, put a bottom in it, put it on your patio, balcony, or fire escape, and you have a mini-greenhouse. It will not give you enough room for a corn crop, but a lot of vegetables and herbs can come out of it.

The bed must be big enough, however, for a soil depth that will hold a full-grown carrot, for instance, without having the top of the green smashed against the glass. If you want tomatoes or squash, they will need room to spread around. It should be apparent that what you will be able to grow and how extensive your garden will be depends almost entirely on the space you have. But a lot of lettuce, radishes, and onions can come out of very little space.

Obviously, if you go so far as to move your mini-greenhouse indoors, you will not require a hot bed. However, you will still need a drain for excess water. You can install a slanting floor in the bottom of the cold frame, but a simpler method is merely to tip it slightly by putting a small object under a corner. When the mini-greenhouse is filled, it should be heavy enough to be steady. The drain can then be nothing more than a small tube in the low corner. The tube can be adapted to whatever sort of container suits your situation.

Greenhouses

If you have the space and really want to become deeply involved in gardening, you may want your own greenhouse. Such greenhouses

The free-standing greenhouse permits light to reach in at any angle

The lean-to greenhouse keeps weather exposure to a minimum

are the best possible artificial environment for starting seeds, propagating cuttings, and growing fresh vegetables and herbs the year round.

There are many greenhouse designs on the market. You can get them designed to mount on foundations or concrete slabs, and some can even be purchased prefabricated, ready for assembly on your site. If you decide to custom-design one for your plot, sketch it out and hand the plan to a competent carpenter for completion.

One of the most popular designs among gardeners who have spent a frigid winter or torrid summer walking back and forth to a greenhouse some distance away is the lean-to type that attaches to the side of your house. If possible, such an addition should face south to get maximum sunlight.

Once you decide to bear the expense of a greenhouse, you can have almost total control of your plants' environment. Warm weather ventilation is easy. All you have to do is open some of the windows. And if they are opened on the lee side of the building, your plants will not be subjected to drafts.

With all the glass in the average greenhouse, you can have windows just about anywhere you want. Many greenhouses even have roof vents for letting air in. A good suggestion is to put the wall vents just above the level of the stands or tables, as this guarantees a free air circulation in hot weather.

In lean-to greenhouses where your home may block off the air, or if you have a lot of hot, still days in your area, you might want a ventilating fan. Put it as high in an end wall as possible. The basic idea of ventilation is to keep hot, humid air moving without causing drafts. Power ventilation should be up where the air is the hottest and the wettest, and as far away from the plants as possible.

When you begin to plan your ventilation needs, take very careful account of the weather where you live. With some memory of the weather and an idea of what you want to grow, you should be able to decide on maximum daytime and minimum nighttime temperatures. You can regulate these temperatures by adjusting the vents manually or you can attach them by a series of levers to a thermostat; then they will open and close as the temperature varies. The thermostat can also turn your vent fan on and off at specified settings. A good garden shop can give you a lot of help in selecting the right equipment if you want to go into this kind of sophistication.

In some parts of interior California (the central valley, for example) and the Southwest, cooling the greenhouse air can be more important in the summer than heating it in the winter. About the most efficient method you can use is one of those old-fashioned air conditioners that cool when a fan sucks the outside air through filters that have water dripping on them.

If you normally have moderate temperature in your area, you probably will not need to burn all that electricity or pay for all that wiring. A good ''damping down'' when it gets really hot will probably be enough. You ''damp down'' your greenhouse by wetting all the paths, ground, benches between the planters, and walls. Another method is to attach a fog nozzle to a hose hung on the wall or from the roof. Systems are available that let you operate the fogger automatically, or it can be done by hand. A fog system will add a lot of cooling with very little expense or effort. In desert areas, it is excellent for humidifying the dry air.

Whatever you do, don't use your house's air-conditioning system. It dries the air and costs a lot to operate, and you may find that you need to add a humidifier to put back moisture the air conditioner has removed.

Either gas heaters or oil burners can be used to heat your greenhouse when it gets cold. With a thermostat, a single duct or burner will probably do the whole job for you. Be sure you vent it to the outside. If you want to, add another zone control to your home heating system and duct it into your greenhouse. If you live in an area with mild winters, you may be able to get by with an electric heater.

In most of California's interior valleys and the rest of the Southwest, shade is one thing you will definitely need. You have probably seen greenhouses with shading paint on the glass. Don't use that approach if you can avoid it. Sooner or later, you will want the sun again and then you have to wait for the paint to wear off or get out and scrape it off yourself.

The alternative is to buy or build yourself a set of wood lath shades. Installed with draw cords along the ridge of the building, such shades can be rolled up or lowered to suit the weather.

If you do have to paint the glass to get shade, be sure you know what paint to use. The stuff you see on greenhouses is not ordinary white paint, which would never wear off. Commercially produced shading compounds are a mixture of lime, water, and a chemical adhesive.

One of the terms you may hear bandied about when you talk about artificial environments is "forcing" plants. Don't let the word confuse you. All "forcing" means is that plants are induced to bloom or bear fruit out of their normal season. Once you start using artificial environments, forcing isn't at all difficult. It simply takes simulating the conditions of the season in which the plant normally bears. The plant won't know the difference.

8 *Indoor Gardening*

By now, if you are one of the growing multitude of apartment and hotel dwellers, you may have decided that vegetable and herb gardening is an avocation to be indulged in only by the suburbanite and his country cousin.

Not so.

And you may have gotten the impression that gardening is year-round work with only a single payday.

Again, not so.

All right, so you live on the twentieth floor. But if you have a balcony, a fire escape, or even a wide window ledge, you have garden space. A lot of food can be raised in the average window box.

If you live in a home that has no outdoor space, or if you insist that the seasons must not stand in the way of your hobby, then you can grow your garden indoors. Plants will grow in flowerpots, in buckets, garbage cans, laundry baskets, practically any container large enough to hold them. All you have to do is make sure that your container is clean and that there are drainage holes either in the bottom or in the sides near the bottom.

Put a couple of inches of gravel in the bottom of your container to facilitate drainage and fill the rest with finely screened topsoil or a

Plants can be grown in containers in a terrace or patio garden

substitute, such as the ones mentioned in the discussion of starting seeds in Chapter III. Plant your vegetables and herbs just as you would in an outdoor garden.

Temperature, watering, feeding, and light will be your major concerns when growing plants in the house. Out of their natural environment, the progress of your plants is totally in your hands.

Basically, you can plan on putting the plants that like cool weather into a room or area where the temperature ranges between 60 and 70 degrees Fahrenheit. Warm-weather plants should be in a spot at 70°F to 80°F.

The best guide for watering your plants is to make sure they are never totally dry. Once the surface in the container dries out to a depth of about a quarter inch, give it more water. Make every effort to keep the soil moist all the way to the bottom of the container. The best way to water plants is to spray them, as the rain does. Your drainage system should take care of excess water, but don't feel free to flood the plants. They will rest about as well in a flooded bed as you would. Worse, in fact, because flooding drives air from the soil and thus drowns the root system and kills the plant.

On the other hand, don't short them to the point that only the surface of the soil is damp. That can sour the ground and kill your plants.

Whether you use topsoil or a soil substitute, about a spoonful of balanced fertilizer per square foot of the soil surface, mixed in well, should keep your plants healthy. Try to apply the fertilizer just before you water.

The main problem with indoor gardening is getting enough light for your plants. One solution, if possible, is to put your plants where the sun will shine on them through a window for a good part of the day. If you are able to give them this kind of light, turn your containers periodically, as the plants will grow toward the light. Some gardeners suggest hanging a light bulb or a fluorescent fixture with a cool white and a warm white tube over the planters.

One way to solve some of your light problems is to limit yourself to plants that prosper with relatively little light. Lettuce and other leafy vegetables require less light than root crops such as radishes, or fruit-bearing crops like tomatoes and peppers. Chives, garlic, parsley, and shallots will thrive inside with a minimum of light. Practically any vegetable or herb that does not require full sun throughout the day is a likely prospect for indoor growing.

Even if you suffer a severe shortage of light, you can still sprout roots. Asparagus, beets, rhubarb, turnips, and the delicacy Belgian endive are all candidates for sprouting.

Belgian endive is the leaf grown from the roots of the witloof chicory. Chicory can be grown from seed, but since its culture requires large amounts of compost, it isn't a pleasant indoor companion. If, however, you can get some chicory root from a friendly outdoor gardener or a garden shop, you are in business.

The best container for endive is a nail keg. Bore it for drainage and fill it as you would another planter, leaving 8 or 9 inches of the keg empty at the top. Cut the roots to about 7 inches long, push them

NAIL KEG

PAPER

SAWDUST

Endive (Approx 7" long)

SOIL

DRAINAGE

Plan of a nail-keg planter for growing endives. Soil is used to root the plants, sawdust permits the plant to grow in a supporting medium

into the ground until only their tops show, and water them heavily. Fill the rest of the keg with sand or sawdust to about an inch from the top and cover it with enough paper to keep out all the light.

In about a month the shoots will break through the cover layer. Then push the covering material aside, cut off the sprouts at the root, cover the roots again, and you'll have another crop of sprouts.

Sprout beets and turnips by planting them about an inch beneath the soil surface in a box or planter. They should be 2 or 3 inches apart. Keep the soil damp. The box can be kept in any convenient spot, even the basement.

Rhubarb and asparagus sprouting again requires a root source. If you can separate a friend from one of these long-living roots, make sure they are exposed to the cold for a while before you plant them again. Rhubarb will be better if it has experienced freezing weather. Try a short spell in your refrigerator. Plant either root in a half-and-half mixture of soil and compost. Keep the rhubarb watered and dark for about 2 months, and the stalks will be ready to eat. Treat

The convenience of window-box tomatoes in the kitchen is worth the extra effort it takes to grow them indoors

asparagus the same way, but put it in a light place or hang a light bulb over it.

Growing tomatoes indoors, especially the small cherry tomatoes, isn't difficult, though it is harder than growing them in the garden. A window box, lots of light, careful feeding, and pollination by hand or brush (wind and insects accomplish outside what you must do indoors) should bring a reasonable crop of this popular vegetable.

Whether you decide to liven up your home with vegetable planters or herb pots, make sure you get a container large enough to do the job. When you are browsing through the huge array of decorative planters on the market, pick the design you like and then buy the next size larger than you think you'll need.

If you have chosen herbs for indoor growing, you will find they often bring the additional pleasure of outdoor aromas inside your home.

The problems of growing herbs indoors are much the same as

getting any plant to produce outside its normal environment. Treat herbs much as you would outdoor vegetables you are growing inside. About the only special treatment herbs require is that their air be kept sufficiently moist to keep down the dust.

Outdoor air usually contains more humidity than that inside your house or apartment, especially in the winter when you heater is going. Moisture in the air attracts dust and keeps it off plants to a large extent; the breeze helps keep them dusted, and the rain washes them. You get none of this indoors.

To prevent layers of dust from settling on your herbs—or other house-grown plants for that matter—give them a periodic dusting. Using a mister—an atomizer or pump bottle—spray the plants with a fine water mist. If you have plants with broad leaves, wash them with a damp sponge.

If your plants are in the same room with a heater or a heating outlet, you can do them a lot of good by putting a humidifier or even a bowl of water on or near the heater for evaporation into the room air.

Remember: you aren't spending your effort merely to test the ability of your plants to survive. Both herbs and vegetables will frequently thrive in less than ideal conditions. But the more effort they put into survival, the less they will put on your table. And what they do produce will be of lesser quality.

Hydroponics

There are conceivable circumstances in which you could not or would not want a soil-filled planter with its fertilizer and moisture drainage in your home or apartment. But don't let that bar you from growing an indoor garden. You can still try hydroponics—growing plants in a chemical solution.

The first thing you must forget is all the stories you have heard about producing monster plants in chemicals. No matter how hard you go at it, you aren't going to get 6-inch tomatoes or anything else you could not get in fertile soil.

The tank arrangement is one of the key factors in hydroponics.

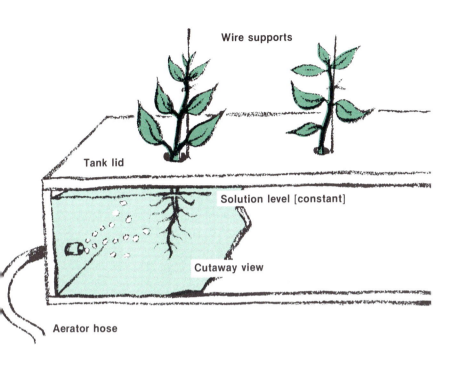

Wire supports

Tank lid

Solution level [constant]

Cutaway view

Aerator hose

A hydroponic tank setup. Basically, the solution is simply a disease-free substitute for good nutrient soil

The container should be as opaque as possible and have a lid that admits little or no light. Plant roots perform better in the dark.

Whether you raise them yourself or buy them, your hydroponic garden will have to be started with seedlings. The roots go through the holes in the tank lid so they are immersed in the nutrient solution. And since the roots will find no solid medium in which to anchor and provide support for the plants, you will have to arrange a system of rods or wires on the tank top to hold the plants erect. Also, you must put an aquarium pump or other means of aeration in the tank solution to resupply the oxygen taken out by the growing plants.

The growing solution should be kept at the same level at all times and changed every couple of weeks as the plants draw out the nutrients.

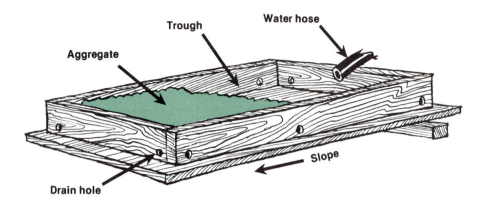

Another hydroponic tank setup

Another method of growing plants without natural soil is to put them in tanks filled with sand, gravel, peat, vermiculite, or some other sterile medium.

If you decide on this method of gardening indoors, your container should have a drain in the bottom so you can pour the nutrient solution through it several times a day. Your goal is to keep the tank filler damp all the time. The excess drains off into a catch basin under the drain and can be poured through again later. As with the liquid method, change the solution every couple of weeks. This system has the advantage of eliminating the contraptions needed to support your plants. The roots will hold in the tank filler.

The nutrient solution you use in hydroponic gardening is a complex mixture of phosphates, sulfates, and nitrates. You don't need detailed knowledge of its makeup as long as you buy or mix it with the advice of a competent garden shop operator or county agent.

Keep in mind that the solution has a pH just like the soil and

106

Indoor lighting used as a growing aid for plants. The tubes provide the correct combination of incandescent and fluorescent rays for plant health

should be kept at the same level all the time. Control of pH is easier with a hydroponic solution than with soil.

What crosses the minds of few gardeners is that you can grow a hydroponic garden outdoors. If you have a patio or balcony that will hold the tanks, this method will save you the problem of providing light for your artificial garden.

If you do not have the outdoor space, talk to your garden shop operator, county agent, or state extension service about what artificial lights are available to substitute for sunlight. There are several on the market, but you will need advice on how many you should have, how far they should be from your plants, and how many hours you should leave them on. Answers to these questions will depend on what you are growing and the size of your project.

If you can, try to keep the temperature around your sensitive plants between 60° and 80°F. You can keep it 10° cooler for hardy plants.

107

You should look into indoor gardening if you are one of the increasing number of Americans who want to grow things but have little or no space. If you decide to try it, remember you are growing living things away from their natural surroundings. The project can be a great challenge for you, and success can be very gratifying. To be successful, however, do all you can to imitate the natural conditions under which the plants you have chosen normally grow. This will mean taking greater care with the details of gardening than might be expected if your plants were in normal surroundings.

But don't let that scare you off. It isn't all that difficult. The conditions described here outline ideal surroundings for ideal results. If your situation, surroundings, or procedures are not perfect, but approach optimum conditions more or less closely, you will probably still get a garden that will make you proud of your efforts.

9 Planting and Transplanting

By now, your soil has been tested. You know what treatment it will need. You know what you can and want to grow. You know how to protect your crops and you know how to get your specific plants off to a good start when the seeds or seedlings go into the ground.

Still, you need to know something more about preparing the soil for your plants and a few of the more exotic methods of getting plants started.

To prepare the soil, no matter what you are planting or how you start the plants, put any humus, building material, filler, fungicide, or fertilizers you need from the beginning on the ground before you start breaking it. Push your spade/turning fork straight down into the ground to its full depth, 8 to 12 inches. Turn the ground completely over, drop it back into the hole, and break up the clods. Keep this up until the entire plot is roughly broken.

Your next step is to rake the ground a small section at a time until all clods are crumbled and the plot is relatively level. Rocks and clods that can't be broken up with your rake should be removed. And now is a good time to add a top dressing if you plan to use one.

Seeds will go into furrows made with your hoe. The traditional method, and one of the best ways to keep your rows straight, is to mark the line with string tied between two stakes, then follow the string with your hoe.

Depending on what you are planting, you might want to put the plants in hills, which are nothing more than rough circles of plants about a foot in diameter. The spacing of your plants in the rows or hills and how deep you put them depends on what you plan to grow.

Once your hill or row is planted, rake the dirt over it, tamp it down gently, and water with a fine mist if the ground is dry. This is the best time to apply your slug and snail bait if these pests are a problem in your area.

The ideal planting temperatures are between 60 and 80 degrees during the day and between 50 and 60 degrees at night, which will give you a daytime soil temperature of at least 50 degrees. In hot climates, this usually means planting on a cloudy day or providing new plants with some shade until they get established.

In the low desert, and in many other California areas, this temperature condition makes fall gardening possible. In such areas the equable fall climate provides a good way to avoid the blistering days of summer and still have home-grown vegetables and herbs.

Obviously, your best fall gardening bets are the cool-weather vegetables. Mid to late September is usually the best time to plant. If there is some chance of frost in your area, you might want to get your plants in earlier, as your main concern is to get your fall garden well established before the first risk of a killing frost. In no-frost areas, you can plant pretty much at your pleasure.

As you probably gathered from the earlier explanation of hardening-off, transplanting is a shock to young plants. To lessen the blow, prepare your garden plot as you would for any planting, and water your flats or pots the day before you plan to move them into the plot. Try to keep the roots covered in soil as they are moved.

You can facilitate the removal of plants from flats by tipping the flat up on one end, giving it a sharp rap against the ground. The entire soil mass will shift to one end of the flat, leaving space to get a trowel, spatula, or putty knife under the seedlings. Cut out a block of soil around the plant, much as you would cut a sheet cake, and lift

Removal of seedlings from planting flat

the square, plant and all, out of the flat. Put the whole block into the ground, filling around it and covering it with garden soil.

If you started your seeds (or bought your seedlings) in metal, paper, or plastic cans, the best way to transplant them is to split the can on both sides and break it away, leaving the soil-and-root ball intact. In some cases, you may find the root system crowded in a ball. If so, loosen the bottom roots with a dull knife, a pointed stick, or a kitchen fork.

Again, you should make a hole in the ground large enough to accept the soil ball as well as the plant's root system. Before you put in the plant, fill the hole with water and wait for it to drain off. Put in the plant and enough soil so that the hole is about half full and water it again. Now fill the hole to the top with soil.

Use of these methods will make it unlikely that your plants will suffer any shock. You can be sure of no-shock transplanting if you started or bought your seedlings in a peat or pressed fertilizer pots. If your plants are in this kind of container, all you have to do is plant it with the seedling. It will break up under the pressure of the growing roots and will help get the plants started by improving the soil around it.

A good rule of thumb for getting transplanted vegetables and herbs off to a good start is to plant them slightly deeper than they were growing in their artificial environment. Also, give them a mist watering after the ground has been firmed around the plants. A good way to get your garden off to a flying start is to mix a weak fertilizer solution with the water.

If you plan to use a mulch, you can apply it as soon as your plants are in. Unless the weather is cloudy, it is also good to give your newly installed plants some shade for their first few days in the garden. A piece of newspaper on a stake where it will block the sun, or a plastic berry box over the plants for two or three days, should be sufficient.

Where it is impossible to give them any shade, you can help plants get started by watering them with a fine mist for two or three days. Planting in the evening is another alternative to keep new transplants out of the sun until they settle down.

To get plants out of clay pots, put your fingers across the top of the pot with the plant between your index and middle fingers. Hold

Knocking out. A sharp rap loosens soil and plant and the whole potful slides out into the protecting hand

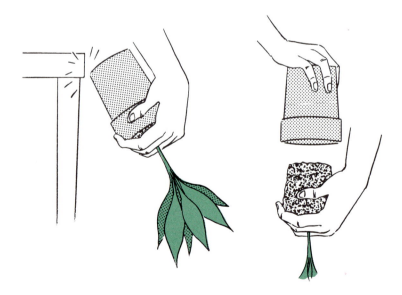

the bottom with your other hand, turn the pot upside down, and now rap the bottom edge of the pot against a hard surface. The root ball and soil should come out more or less in one piece.

If the formerly potted plant is destined for the garden, plant it much as you would plants from flats or cans.

Plants that are being moved to larger containers as part of your indoor garden must get slightly different treatment. Once the soil-and-root ball is out of the pot you should cut off any roots that have wrapped around the ball. Score the ball about an eighth to a quarter of an inch deep down its sides before putting it into its new pot.

Be sure your new pots are clean. If they are clay pots, soak them in water an hour or so before using, just as you did earlier.

Prepare the gravel or filler base of the pot as you did before and fill the pot to the point that the surface of the old soil ball will be about an inch below the lip of the new pot. Pack the soil well with a blunt stick or your hands, put in the ball, and fill in around it with more soil. Pack the full pot with your fingers and water it until both the old and the new soil are saturated.

Spray the repotted plants with insecticide and keep them in the shade for a few days.

For perennial vegetables and herbs, you will probably be more successful in growing new plants if you forget about the seeds and seedlings and turn to division.

Every year, a perennial grows in diameter, adding new roots and stems to the outer edge of the plant clump. After two or three years this growth can get so big that the plants become crowded, and some begin to lose out in competition with others. You can increase your stock by simply digging up the entire root-stem bundle and dividing it into separate plants. Each new plant should have its share of roots and stems. Sometimes, you can merely pull the separate plants apart. In other cases, you will have to use a knife or blade to cut them into different plants. However you do it, all each new plant requires to survive and thrive is a crown or stem and a root or the rudiment of a root.

The best times to divide perennials are early spring and fall, when the plants are dormant. If you find that the center of the clump has become weak and woody, you may want to throw it away and replant only the fresh outer stock. Always keep the plants moist when they are out of the ground, and replant as soon as possible.

The most important factor in dividing and transplanting perennials is speed. If you cannot transplant them the same day they are divided, put the plants in an out-of-the-way place and cover them with damp soil. You can keep them fresh by covering them with wet burlap or wet them and wrap them in plastic. Be on guard against the roots drying out before you get them transplanted.

For many perennial herbs, layering is another way of increasing your stock without seeds or seedlings. All you have to do with an

Soil layering. The cut, kept from healing, is covered with soil and develops roots. The new plant is later separated

herb such as rosemary is find a branch near the ground and plant it. If you do this properly, it will give you a whole new plant. Pick a growing young branch that is flexible enough to bend without breaking. Make a diagonal cut halfway through the branch about a foot from its end, just below one of the nodes, and insert a pebble or some object to keep the cut open. Plant the branch in a four- to six-inch-deep hole without detaching it from the parent plant. Tack it in place with a heavy wire loop that straddles the branch and tie the end of the branch still out of the hole to a vertical stake. Then fill the hole with a half-and-half mixture of soil and either sand or peat, and put a brick or heavy stone over the buried branch to keep the ground firm and to hold in moisture.

It will take six weeks or more for most perennials to take root. To check on how it is progressing, simply scratch away the soil and look to see what's happening. When the new roots are growing well, cut the stem to the parent plant just below the first cut.

If you plan to move your new herb to another spot, you can plant the layered section in a soil-filled box. Once you cut the contact to the parent, it can be transplanted anywhere.

Early spring is the best time to layer plants, but in freeze-free climates layering can succeed at any time of the year. If you live in an area that may receive a hard frost, apply a layer of mulch over the layered area.

Some herbs—sage, thyme, and savory among them—will actually form small clumps of roots whenever a branch touches the ground. You can cut these rooted sections away from the parent plant and transplant them with good results. Mint and other such plants form roots at the joints of their runners; these can be taken off and transplanted. You can start new lavender, southernwood, lavender cotton, rosemary, and some other herbs by planting such stem cuttings. When you cut off a side shoot for replanting, trim it to about 4 to 6 inches long. Take some of the main stem heel with it and trim off the lower leaves on the cutting.

Whether you start the cutting in a pot, can flat, or the garden itself, the main thing you must insure is that there are no air spaces around its roots. If there are, it probably won't grow. Put about half the stem into the ground and pack the soil tight enough so that you can tweak the plant without breaking it out. Check your new plantings now and then to make sure they are still firmly in place. Always water after insertion to settle and firm the ground.

Cuttings are usually best planted in the early summer, but they can be planted almost any time in frost-free climates. In colder areas, you can plant them with good results from early spring to fall as long as they have a chance to get started before the first killing frost.

With all the seeds and seedlings available these days, it may seem slightly silly to go to all of the trouble of making cuttings or layering and dividing plants. On the other hand, economy is one of the reasons you started a garden in the first place. Every plant you get through one of these methods is one you did not have to buy.

Even a better reason for these methods is to insure continuation of a particular plant strain you really like or that is well suited to your plot. They abolish the risks of the wrong seeds for your situation, of cross-pollination that produces poor second-generation plants, and the problems that go with starting seeds.

10 *Feeding, Watering, Weeding*

In the last few years the subject of fertilizing the nation's food crops has fallen into a mass of confusion. It sometimes seems as if government agencies find another dangerous element in our diet every week. There are charges that the synthetic fertilizers we use to grow our crops produce nothing but worthless roughage that fills our stomachs but does not nourish our bodies. On this wave of concern have come the so-called "organic" or "natural" gardeners to add a new dimension to gardening.

Basically, to decide how your garden will be fed, you should know something about chemical fertilizers, manure, compost, and so-called green manure, and their application.

Commercial Fertilizers

Probably the most common fertilizers you will find on the market are the manufactured liquid or dry fertilizers. They come in two general types, "complete" and specialized. A commercial fertilizer is considered complete when it contains the three essential plant food elements: nitogren, phosphorus, and potassium. Nurserymen and fertilizer dealers refer to these elements by their chemical symbols: N, P, and K, respectively.

Fish Emulsion
Fertilizer 5-2-2
A. B. C.

NON-BURNING • 100% FISH, DEODORIZED

The numbers that often appear on plant food labels indicate the proportion of ingredients in the complex. In this typical house plant food, (A) 5 stands for nitrogen, a leaf growth stimulator; (B) 2 represents phosphorus, for root hardiness; and (C) 2 indicates potash, which aids assimilation of the nutrients by the plant

Commercial fertilizers have a series of numbers—5 - 10 - 5 or 10 - 20 - 5—on the labels which tell you the percentage of each of the essential elements they contain. Once your soil has been tested and you know what you want to grow, and with a little advice from your extension agent or local nurseryman, you should have no difficulty picking a ''complete'' commercial fertilizer that will suit your needs.

Specialized plant foods are usually acid plant foods or are fertilizers high in content of one or two of the basic elements and deficient in at least one nutrient.

Basically, about all you need to know of the elements in commercial fertilizer is that nitrogen promotes growth; phosphorus makes for strong root systems, promotes early maturity, boosts the vitamin content of the plants, and increases yields; and potassium makes vigorous roots, helps make bigger yields of better quality root crops, helps plants resist disease and retain better color and storage quality.

To guard against some potentially harmful side effects of commercial fertilizer, you should be aware of the difference between non-protein organic, inorganic, and organic protein types.

The two non-protein organic fertilizing compounds—urea and calcium cyanamid—are man-made carbon compounds that dissolve easily in water, contain a high degree of nitrogen, but leave no humus building material in the plot.

Inorganic fertilizers are manufactured from minerals. Nitrogen, which is a gas in its pure form, may be in the form of nitrate of soda or sulfate of ammonia, while phosphorus appears as phosphoric acid and potassium as potash. It is not essential for you to understand the complex chemical-biological activity that takes place in the soil to convert these minerals into the form plants can use. But you should know that they can leave salts in the soil that may damage clayey or naturally salty ground. Commercial fertilizers' main advantages are the high concentrations of the three elements they contain and the speed with which these elements become usable in the soil.

In many of the inorganic fertilizers you will find the salt residue problem partly solved by the nitrogen being in non-protein or protein organic form.

Protein organic fertilizers are made from animal slaughterhouse and vegetable residues. They are usually used to contribute nitrogen, but those containing bone residue will provide some phosphate and potash. The dried blood and bone meal in these fertilizers will produce some humus, but not enough to have a marked impact on soil conditions. If your ground is acid, damp most of the time, or cool, there may not be enough bacterial activity to break down these fertilizers. And unless this breakdown occurs, your plants cannot use the nitrogen they contain.

The organic fertilizers have gained a reputation for being slow to act. In some cases you may find that to be an advantage, because they tend to be longer lasting than synthetics and inorganic forms. But the speed of their action depends largely on how finely they are ground and the condition of the soil before they are applied. Their nutrients become available very quickly in warm, moist, well-limed ground.

Manure

The most complete of the organic fertilizers is manure. Its

content of nutrient elements will vary with the animals from which it comes and the diet they have been on. Whatever its source, manure is never as rich as commercial fertilizers. A typical ratio is 1 - 1 - 1, flat even in the ratio of essential elements and low in each. Despite this deficiency, manures are very valuable for your garden because they are high in the organic matter—40 percent and higher—that keeps the soil open and workable and makes phosphorus available to your plants.

In general, old manure that has been piled up and left alone for several months will release its nutrients quicker and easier than fresh manure. A good rule of thumb is to expect 8 to 10 pounds of nitrogen, about the same amount of potash, and roughly 6 pounds of phosphoric acid per ton of cattle manure. Good horse manure will almost double these figures, while pig manure will usually be less nutritious than cattle manure. Fowl manure will have 400 or 500 percent more nitrogen than that from cattle, will double or triple its phosphorus content, and is about equal in potash. You should use poultry manure with care since it makes clay stickier and adds acid to the soil.

Application

Fertilizers should always be applied according to the instructions on the label. If there are no instructions, you will generally be right to give your plants a starter fertilizer application when they are planted and a nitrogen or complete fertilizer application after they are growing well. Give your perennials another application in the fall.

Your first application should be the heaviest and should be worked into the soil. The food can be applied by spreading it over the entire plot before the garden is planted or by banding—putting fertilizer in a ditch between the vegetable rows and covering these strips with soil. The second application can be put on as a side-dressing—spreading the fertilizer alongside or around your plants and working it into the soil.

However the fertilizer is applied, the area should be watered thoroughly once the fertilizer is on it. Plants cannot absorb the dry fertilizer and it can burn seeds or plants if it touches them.

Another way of feeding your plants is by spraying them with a mixture of water and diluted fertilizer, foliar feeding. This system is a good way of supplying minor nutrients to your plants in California's warmer areas and is a superior way for you to feed your plants if your plot is sandy or heavily leached.

Get all the advice you can before you start applying fertilizers. Too little, and rain or watering can leach it away quickly and leave you with spindly, poor-producing plants. Too much will make them barren and may kill your vegetables and herbs.

Peat and spent hops are both good soil conditioners but are low in usable nutrients for soil. Seaweed, on the other hand, will provide your plants with as much nitrogen as cattle manure and triple the potash.

Green manure

If you have a large garden, you may want to try green manuring. This is nothing more than planting part of your plot in a cover crop, letting it grow, and then digging it into the soil to rot. Green manuring is a long-term way of rehabilitating and building soil. Unless you plant a leguminous crop such as lupine, cowpeas, or soybeans, you can expect the nitrogen content of the plot to drop at first as you use the ground. Nitrogen is used up as the greenery breaks down. Legumes, however, have their own nitrogen nodes that are enough to keep the soil's nitrogen content up.

You may find that green manuring is not for your garden since it takes at least a couple of months from the time the cover crop is turned under until you can plant the area. And that, only when your land is well drained, your soil is not acid, you add a nitrogen activator when you turn it under, and the soil is warm.

Compost

Composting is another technique you should be aware of but may not be able to use. The compost is made at home by piling up all kinds of vegetation, coffee grounds, and wet newspapers, and letting

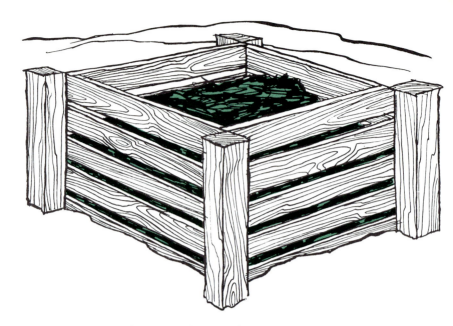

A compost heap. Building a container of slats keeps the pile within bounds and permits air circulation

it all rot into a crumbling brown substance much like humus. Compost heaps are usually built in layers, each layer sprinkled with manure or a commercial activator and soil. If you want a heap large enough to treat a quarter-acre plot, it should be about 3 feet square. Don't get the idea that a compost heap is the same thing as a pile of weeds. In a well-made heap, the temperature will rise to nearly 180 degrees as bacteria break down the vegetable matter. When its contents are ready to use, the pile will cool.

If you decide to build a compost pile, be sure the material is moist when it goes in. If it is dry, water it lightly. Keep out woody material and break up big chunks such as cabbage stumps. Cap the heap with a layer of soil to keep in the heat, and make the top dish-shaped to catch the rain. You can build the heap and pull it out to widen it when it reaches the desired height or drive a rod into the complete heap to help aeration.

Your compost heap will be ready for use about six months after it is completed. It will provide about the same nutrients to your soil as good manure.

Before you decide on either manure or compost for your garden, give a thought to your neighbors. Neither manure nor compost is the best way to keep friends in an urban neighborhood. Both give off a pungent aroma that the people next door may not appreciate.

Weeds

Once your garden is fertilized, mulched, planted, and growing, you will find that you are growing more than you planned—weeds.

There are many ways of dealing with your weed crop. You can dig them or pull them. You can spray them or shade them out. Or you can let them grow.

The idea of letting weeds grow along with your vegetables and herbs was developed by some of the ''natural'' gardeners who have come forth in recent years. They argue that the weeds anchor the soil, attract insects that would otherwise eat your producing plants, act as homes for beneficial insects, help keep the soil loose, and aid garden growth in other ways.

But even these gardeners acknowledge that too many weeds are a threat to vegetables. The simplest method of getting the weeds out of your garden is to pull them by hand. If you use this method, arm yourself with a small digging tool to help with the deep-rooted varieties. Watering the plot a few days before you plan your attack will help by loosening the roots' hold on the ground. Try to avoid pulling large weeds growing near your vegetables as their roots may be entwined with your crop and pulling may bring out both plants.

Probably the most common method of dealing with weeds is hoeing. Any sharp hoe will cut the weed off at or just below ground level. When you go shopping for a hoe and find yourself facing an apparently endless variety of sizes and shapes, simply keep in mind your particular needs and the hoeing technique with which you feel most comfortable. However you go about this chore, arrange your work so that you approach the weed you are planning to cut rather than trampling it into the ground as you back along the rows.

If you take up the hoe as your weapon in the war against weeds, try to disturb the soil as little as possible. Attempt to just scrape the invaders off at ground level. Digging any deeper might contribute to soil leaching, or your hoe might even cut the shallow roots of your vegetables.

Hoeing weeds will not kill them immediately. Eventually, however, the constant cutting will kill even the most persistent weed. If you are impatient, you can coat the cut end of a persistent weed with herbicide or a strong mixture of water and rock salt (you will have to boil the water to dissolve the salt). That weed will not be back.

An effective method of clearing weeds out of your garden without the repeated effort that hoeing requires is shading them out. A good layer of mulch will retard weed growth and keep many weed seeds from germinating. Covering a weed with tar paper or another air-and-light-proof material and sealing the edges by burying them in the soil will make a weed overheat. The heat and lack of sun will kill it.

You don't need much knowledge of chemical weed killers to use them properly. You must know, however, how they work. One variety kills all vegetation it touches, but it must touch a plant before it will work. Another type lies in the soil and kills seeds as they sprout, and there is one that sterilizes the soil for a period of from several months to a number of years. Finally, there are chemicals that clean all vegetation and seeds out of the soil for up to a month.

You can get herbicides to the weeds via tank sprayers, watering cans, or attachments to your garden hose, among other ways. It makes little difference which way you choose as long as you guard against the potentially disastrous effects these powerful chemicals can have. Be sure that your delivery system takes the herbicide to the weed—but nowhere else. Always follow the label directions on a herbicide container to the letter.

Watering

There are all sorts of systems designed to water your garden. You can get sprinklers and soakers, portable systems and sophisticated built-ins. The kind you choose will depend on how much you are willing to spend. Sprinklers are a good method of getting water to your garden; they are the closest artificial simulation of rain. The main drawback to a sprinkler is the water lost through evaporation, especially in hot, dry weather. If you decide to use a sprinkler, make sure it has a spray pattern that will cover your entire plot uniformly.

French irrigation—flooding prepared ditches between the rows of plants—and canvas or plastic soakers that attach to a garden hose deliver the water directly into the ground around the plants. The trench system is best suited if you have a large garden and plan to keep it arranged the same way through many seasons.

The amount of water your garden will need is directly related to your soil. Clay can absorb about three times as much water as sand and will hold it like a sponge. You will have to water sandy ground more often.

Aside from the watering necessary when you fertilize your vegetable garden, it will need approximately an inch of water a week. This amount will insure that the root zone of the plot—a foot to 18 inches below the surface—is kept moist. To make sure this zone is damp, it is a good idea to get yourself a soil probe or an auger. Pushing one of these into the soil will bring you a sample of the subsurface soil Another method, if you use a sprinkler, is to purchase a moisture indicator. Attached to the system, it will turn the water on and then off as the ground reaches a specific degree of dampness.

Earlier we mentioned that sandy soil requires more watering as a rule than clay or loam. In the chapter on soils, we indicated that the already excessive salts present in sandy, arid soils can be made worse by watering. At first glance, this would suggest a ''damned if you do, damned if you don't'' situation in many desert or semi-arid areas. The best way to avoid the problem is to water with a vengeance. Large amounts of water leach mineral salts out of loose ground.

If your garden plot is sandy and your climate dry, start your season—before you plant—by giving your land 6 inches to 2 feet of water for every foot of depth you want to leach. The exact amount of water you will need at first depends on how salty your soil is and how much you need to leach out.

It is a good idea to discuss your irrigation plans with your county agent or nurseryman in advance, but plan on what appears to be excessive irrigation throughout the growing season. The large amounts of water will leach out salts earlier waterings left in the soil and keep the salt level within tolerable limits.

The best time to water is early in the morning or evening. The sun is not as hot and therefore you reduce the amount of water lost through evaporation. You can avoid many fungus growths by watering your plants early enough in the evening to insure that the leaf surfaces are dry before nightfall.

You should also avoid giving your garden several light waterings rather than a single soaker. Light sprinklings will merely wet the surface and can cause roots to seek the surface or form shallow systems.

11 Disease and Pest Control

Shortly after you get involved with vegetable and herb gardening, you will find that you have some unexpectedly friendly neighbors. Even in the most urban areas, you may find that moles, gophers, mice, and other small animals have survived very well in the midst of the city. And you may be surprised at the wide range of insect varieties that seem to thrive in any locale. The presence of your garden could introduce you to whole new worlds of fungi and plant infections.

If your efforts are to end in results, you should know the methods of preventing or removing these unwanted visitors. In most instances, preventing them is a lot easier than later cures.

Animal Pests

One of the most common garden-damaging animals in California, and many western areas, is the gopher. About the only sure way of keeping these persistent little diggers out of your plot is to plant a rabbit-wire fence 10 to 24 inches into the ground all around the garden.

If you find one of the telltale dirt piles where a gopher has cleaned out his tunnels, you can trap him by digging a trench across

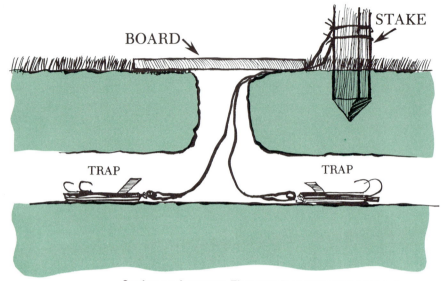

Setting gopher traps. The stake is to prevent the animal from escaping, trap and all.

his burrow and putting a trap in the burrow on each side of the ditch. Cover the trench with boards, leaving enough gaps to permit the gopher to come running to repair his tunnel. Be sure to tie the trap to a stake outside the tunnel so you can retrieve it.

Traps will not be enough to get rid of a heavy gopher infestation. If you think you have a lot of gophers, poison them. First, locate their tunnel by probing with the handle of a broom or a hoe. When your probe breaks through, drop the poisoned bait through the hole and close it up. You can buy commercially prepared poison baits or prepare your own by dosing cut potatoes, sweet potatoes, beets, or other vegetables with strychnine or thallium sulfate.

Probably the most challenging method of getting rid of a gopher or any other burrow dweller is to dig into the burrow. then slide a fifteen- or twenty-foot length of water hose as far into the burrow as you can. Using a funnel, pour a little gasoline into the hose and blow through the hose as hard as you can. After several such blasts in quick succession, the gasoline fumes in the burrow should become unbearable to the animal. Your varmint can be captured in a gunny-sack or dispatched with a shotgun as he surfaces.

The challenge in this method is being fast enough to catch the visitor. Many burrow dwellers will be on their way out within thirty seconds of the time you finish the operation. You may also be surprised at what you catch. In addition to gophers, groundhogs, and ground squirrels, skunks or snakes may be in your bag.

If you merely want the burrower to abandon his work for other parts, simply plug the hole when he has been forced out. Kerosene or concentrated sulfur spread around the hole will discourage his return.

Although moles are usually meat-eaters, they can still do serious damage to your plot with their constant burrowing and disruption of root and drainage systems. Moles can be poisoned using the same methods used for gophers; there are also numerous traps on the market that will put an end to their digging. Since the moles' main foods are grubs and worms, one good way to get them to abandon your plot is to treat the ground with Chlordane 10-G or some other pesticide designed to get rid of grubs and worms. The same kind of fence you sink for gophers will also provide a mole barrier.

If all else fails, you can get rid of a persistent mole by ramming a spade into his tunnel approximately a foot behind its most advanced point. With its retreat thus blocked, you can dig the mole out if you move fast.

You can best handle an invasion of ground squirrels as you would gophers. Opossums are easily trapped with either steel traps or harmless metal box traps baited with fish or dogfood. Rabbits, raccoons, and squirrels are kept away best by your active dog or cat, or your gun. Woodchucks can be easily exterminated with gas cartridges being currently produced. And many poisoned baits are available that will rid your garden of mice and rats.

If you live in an area with a considerable deer population, you have a difficult problem. There are nasty-tasting chemical repellents available, but they are good only for winter protection. They should not be applied during the summer to plants you are going to eat.

Other than these, your only choice is to build a fence. If you decide to do this, the fence should be electrified and at least 8 feet high, or it should have an 8-foot outrigger attached to its top.

Your best protection against birds is a wire or cheesecloth shield that fits over the plants themselves or the whole plot. Some gardeners have had success frightening away birds with strips of foil or reflectors tied so they will flutter in the breeze. Scarecrows sometimes provide temporary protection.

One of the easiest methods of discouraging many small animal pests is to encourage the presence of other animals. Cats are effective in getting rid of birds, moles, gophers, squirrels, and chipmunks. Dogs will deter many small animals, and harmless snakes will eat insects, gophers, moles, and mice. Skunks also eat mice, along with cutworms, grubs, and grasshoppers, as do weasels and shrews.

Insects

A fact you may or may not be aware of is that insects are the most numerous form of life on earth. They are everywhere in all sorts of varieties, and as soon as your plants begin coming up it may seem that all of them have dropped in on your plot for a visit and a snack.

Your defense against insect invasion starts when you buy your plants. Be sure you purchase them from a reputable firm that has a reputation to protect and will take pains to insure that its product is healthy.

It's important that you keep your garden clean. Burn sick plants, keep the trash cleared away, and get rid of most weeds. Rotate your crops to insure that a particular bug does not infest an entire section of your garden, and turn soil that is not being used to expose pests hiding in the ground.

Timing your planting can be important in limiting insect damage. Many insects appear at specific times of the year. If your county agent or nurseryman can tell you when to expect them, you can delay planting until they are gone and save a lot of headaches.

The attack of insect armies may come on many fronts. There are insects that attack roots, stems, and foliage. Some do their work in daylight; others strike at night. Some insects will even help others in their assault. Many ants that are harmless to plants will protect aphids from their enemies and carry them from one plant to another to get the honeydew they produce.

There are all sorts of ways you can counter insect attacks. Until recently, many gardeners almost automatically reached for the insecticide sprayer or duster when they went out after insects. As a result of the environmental movement, a more balanced view of insect control has come to gardening, a view that recognizes many possible methods of solving an insect problem.

Earlier, methods of discouraging bird invasions were discussed. There is, however, something to be said for attempting to attract birds that do not eat your vegetables. Making available bird feeders, bird baths, and shrubs and trees for nesting sites will usually bring them. You may be surprised at how many insects they and their young will devour. Bats are good night-flying insect catchers, and a toad or a lizard will eat more than a hundred insects each day.

One insect restraint that has recently become popular is so-called biological control. This basically means pitting one insect against another, the introduction of predatory bugs to get rid of the plant eaters.

Of all the predatory insects the little ladybug (ladybird beetle) has received the most publicity. The three hundred and fifty species of the little spotted beetle are highly prized because they prey on one of the most numerous, widespread, and damaging garden eaters, the aphid. A single beetle will eat up to four hundred aphids a week.

But the ladybug is not alone in her aid to needy gardeners. The aphis lions—dobson flies, ant lions, and lacewings—do an effective job of eradicating insects too. Nocturnal lacewings eat moth eggs, caterpillars, scale insects, aphids, mealybugs, and thrips. The goldeneye lacewing devours aphids, red spiders, and thrips, and ant lions wreak havoc on the ant population. Ambush bugs, assassin bugs, several varieties of spider, the damsel bug, and hover flies are all highly effective insect catchers that will willingly take up residence in your garden. The praying mantis is the most effective of the lot.

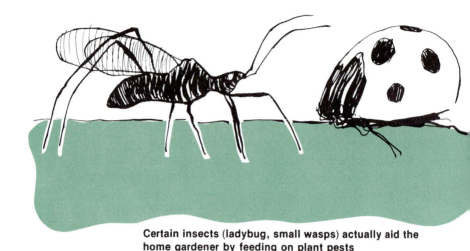

Certain insects (ladybug, small wasps) actually aid the home gardener by feeding on plant pests

This large insect spends his entire life in constant search for aphids, leafhoppers, caterpillars, beetles, and practically any other insect he can find.

You can buy cases of ladybugs for introduction into your plot. Put a little water into each case and keep them in the refrigerator until you are ready for the ladybugs. When you put them out, simply dampen the ground and release the beetles near an aphid infestation. You can also get mantis egg cases in the winter and early spring. Tape them to trees or shrubs about 3 feet above the ground. When the weather warms, the mantises will hatch—usually about midsummer.

If you want to try this biological method of pest control, ask your county agent about recent developments. Several agricultural colleges have been experimenting with wasps the size of gnats. They are harmless to human beings but apparently very effective against their insect victims. If you are a real nature lover, with a wide streak of courage, you can avoid the temptation to discourage normal-size wasps and hornets from moving into your plot.

The major problem with using bugs to combat other bugs is their habit of following the food supply. Once your garden is cleared of the insects your predators eat, they will move to more fertile ground. When they are gone, vegetable eaters from other parts of the neighborhood may move in and there is no guarantee that the predators will come back with them.

If possible, try to use biological controls in as large an area as you can. However, if your neighbors are using heavy chemical applications to control their insects, your predators may be killed off. And once you start with this method, you should avoid any sort of insecticide spraying unless and until you are ready to abandon biological control.

There are several other methods of insect control you might want to try before resorting to insecticides. An extremely strong soap and water solution—about a cup of soap to a gallon of water—will kill aphids when it is sprayed or painted on plants. However, be sure to wash it off after it has done the job since the heavily alkaline solution can also harm your plants.

Sulfur dust will kill some mites, scale insects, and caterpillars, but it will damage squash and cucumbers. Sulfur should not be used when the temperature is above 80 degrees. Mixed with water and sprayed directly on insects, molasses will kill many of them.

A strong stream of water is enough to knock down and drown many insects as well as to injure soft-bodied aphids. Flooding your plot with 3 or 4 inches of water a few days before planting will kill thrips, aphids, and caterpillars.

Spread wood ashes around your onions and cabbages to discourage maggots. Sprayed on plants in solution ashes are said to control aphids and cucumber beetles. Spray skim milk on tomatoes and peppers to eradicate mosaic, which is a virus disease. A spray of mild salt solution will kill some mites and cabbage worms, while crushed eggshells dug in around plants will deter cutworms. Mineral oil dropped onto corn silk where it enters the ear tip will kill corn earworms, but be sure to apply it only after the silk is limp and beginning to turn brown.

Marigolds acting as guard plants

And as we discussed earlier, a mulch of heavy paper spread on the soil will keep many insects from getting to your plants.

You can limit pest damage by planting portions of your plot at intervals—successive planting—so all of a single variety will not mature at once, and by spot planting, spreading the same plant variety in different parts of the garden. You might also put in trap plants that attract insects away from your crop. Then you can kill most of them in one swoop, and if the plant goes too there is no loss. Or you can plant marigolds or other so-called guard plants that repel insects. Tansy, garlic, painted daisies, and many herbs act as guard plants.

134

If it is necessary for you to use insecticides, you should know that they are *not* all more or less alike. Insecticides are divided into those manufactured from plants—botanical controls—and the chemicals developed in laboratories, including the recently much maligned chlorinated hydrocarbons.

Rotenone, pyrethrum, nicotine, garlic, sabadilla, hellebore, and ryania are natural poisons that will destroy insects.

Rotenone is produced from derris, cube, or timbo. Pyrethrum is a combination of toxins from three varieties of chrysanthemums, while nicotine is an ingredient of the tobacco plant. All three are insect contact and stomach poisons. Garlic oil has been found to be an effective mosquito poison; sabadilla seeds produce a poison for leafhoppers, squash bugs, and cabbage worms; and the root of the veratrum produces hellebore, an insect stomach poison. Ryania is an effective treatment against squash bugs, corn borers and earworms, cabbage worms, onion thrips, Japanese beetles, and some aphid varieties.

What happens when you make a solution of compost and water to use as a garden spray is not quite clear, but strained about an hour after it has been mixed it has been known to kill worms on squash and celery.

All of the botanical insect poisons other than nicotine are harmless to human beings and other warm-blooded animals. All are non-persistent: their toxic effects wear off in a matter of hours or days. On the one hand, the non-persistent nature of these insecticides insures that they will do no permanent damage to the environment. On the other, it means you will have to establish a program of periodic spraying to insure that the bugs do not return when the poison wears off.

With the synthetic insecticides, Chlordane, and chlorinated hydrocarbons, you gain the advantages of extremely deadly poisons that will get the bugs present when you spray and stay around to take care of the ones that come later.

With all pesticides, be sure to read all label directions and warnings carefully. Make sure the chemical you are buying will deal with your problem, and don't mix the spray solution any stronger than recommended on the label. The best time to spray an insecticide is mid-morning. That gives the plants time to dry before dark. Try to do your spraying when the temperature is below 85 degrees. Pesticides may damage plants in hotter weather. Try to keep the spray off open blossoms, or it will kill bees and other pollinating insects. If you can, do your spraying when there is no wind. If a breeze does come up, be sure to spray downwind; don't let the spray blow back on you. Also, keep the chemicals off your clothing and skin and don't smoke or eat —in other words, keep your hands away from your mouth—while you are spraying or until you have had a chance to wash thoroughly. While you are mixing, spraying, and putting things away, cover as much of your body as possible, including rubber gloves over your hands. A spray-paint mask is a good idea for your eyes, nose, and mouth. And when you're done change clothes and wash all exposed areas thoroughly.

There are two basic methods of applying insecticide to your garden: liquid spray and dusting. If your pesticide is available in dry form, you may find it more convenient to apply. Don't use the shaker or the pump can in which many dusts are sold. They just won't get the poison to the bugs. Use either a plunger type or a rotary duster with a nozzle attachment that lets you reach the underside of the leaves where the bugs may be hiding.

The main advantages of dusting are the elimination of mixing dry chemicals with water and the ability to leave left-over chemicals in the dusting machine. Dusting's disadvantages include greater expense than spraying and the fact that the dust is easily washed off by rain or watering.

If you decide on a liquid spray, be sure you select one that will do the job. There are sprayers ranging in size from hand-held flit guns to heavy tank sprayers that hold up to 4 or 5 gallons at one filling, and there are models that fit on the end of your garden hose. Be sure to mix a fresh batch of chemical each time you use the sprayer. It is also a good idea to shake or stir the chemicals periodically as you work to keep the solution from separating.

Once you have finished spraying, be sure you wash the spraying equipment thoroughly inside and out. Pump clear water through the nozzle to make sure it is cleaned out, too, then hang it upside down so it will drain dry. Remove the pump so it can be dried also. Close the tank when it is dry so wasps and other insects do not move in. And, most important, don't use the same sprayer for insecticides and herbicides. There are bound to be microscopic traces of herbicide left that can damage your plants when mixed in with the bug poison.

When applying liquid spray, your goal should be to get a fine mist on all parts of the plant to the point of run-off without dripping. With dusts, cover the foliage with a light cloud without leaving a heavy coat of dust on the plants.

Two more recent developments in insect control are systemic poisons and parasites that feed on the problem insects. Systemic controls are usually applied to the soil and are absorbed by plants to wait for insect attack. The bugs eat and are eliminated. Be careful, however; this method can kill plants.

Parasitic control is a very specific method in which a virus, bacterium, or spore that preys on a certain insect is put into the garden. In order for it to be effective, though, you must have a heavy infestation of a single insect.

If you are interested in either of these methods, detailed advice can be obtained through your county agent or nurseryman.

Diseases

Most of the techniques of spot planting, crop rotation, and weeding used to minimize insect invasion of your garden also will help to keep down the threat of plant diseases. When buying plants, always try to get those that are naturally resistant or treated to resist the common diseases in your area, and establish a feeding, watering, and spraying program early to keep your plot healthy. If you do find an infected plant, pull it and burn it without delay.

Speed and planning are important factors in your battle against plant diseases. A well-planned spraying program will keep disease from getting a good start when an infection is present and it will

eliminate the insects that may carry infections from plant to plant.
Many diseases, especially in frames, hot beds, or other
containers, will build up in the soil around infected plants. Since they
often prey on one type of plant, a well-planned crop rotation
program—trying to alternate plants not vulnerable to the same
diseases—can go far to keep your garden healthy. Proper spacing of
your plants and insuring they get enough sun will keep many plants
healthy, too.

There are three categories of disease that can attack your
plants—fungi, bacteria, and viruses. Fungi and bacteria kill your
plants by living off their tissues. They form spores and spread when
they are blown or washed to other plants. Fungus spores form thick
walls in adverse weather and can survive a long time in the plants or
the soil through the worst weather. You can identify some
fungi—mildew among them—by the white powdery growth that
appears on the plants as the parasite's threads and spores spread.
These are easy to spot early and counterattack. Most fungi, however,
penetrate deep into your plants and can be seen only when they send
out spore threads.

Some bacteria too produce spores to winter over, while others
survive by living in dormant plant cells and plant debris.

Virus infection is probably the most difficult sort of disease to
identify. Although the specific method of attack is not known, virus
infections appear to penetrate all parts of a plant through its sap
stream. A virus infection can kill some plants almost immediately
while others will weaken and die very slowly. Keep your eyes open for
stunted growth, mottled patterns on leaves, ring spots on leaves,
curling or misshapen leaves and stems, an abnormal number of
shoots, and breaking flowers as symptoms of virus infections. If the
virus starts after the plant is growing, the existing shoots and leaves
will show few effects. New growth is the place to look for sick
development.

Your greatest enemy in fighting a virus will be the insects.
Aphids, leafhoppers, thrips, mealybugs, whiteflies, and other insects
are known to carry viruses from sick to healthy plants. Of course,

propagating plants by shoots or cuttings will carry over a virus if the original plant was infested. Apparently few viruses endure in the seeds of infected plants, but they can stay in the soil waiting for next year's new plants.

Cheap, weak seeds and seedlings, close spacing, acid soils, bad lighting, overfeeding with synthetic fertilizers, very hot or cool weather, can all encourage the rise of plant disease. Make sure your plot is well drained, has plenty of peat, leaf mold, or other humus-building material. In greenhouses and indoor gardens try to avoid humid, warm, stagnant air conditions that encourage parasites. Soil pasteurization is often a good practice for indoor gardens.

As soon as you have your seedlings in hand, whether you grow them or buy them, check for disease. Cabbages may already show swollen roots as a result of clubroot, or there may be the first growth of scale problems. Practice as much sanitation as possible by keeping your tools clean, washing and disinfecting pots, cold frames, or hot beds periodically. Greenhouses or the interior of closed containers—hot beds or frames—should be washed with hot soapy water annually. Don't forget to scrub the benches and work areas.

There are several chemicals on the market for sterilizing, or pasteurizing, your potting soil. Most of them contain large amounts of formaldehyde. If you want to mix your own, add approximately one tablespoon of chemical to five tablespoons of water. That will be enough to sprinkle one flat thoroughly. Let the container sit covered around the clock before planting. If you treat larger amounts of soil, they may have to stand for a month or more before they can be planted. Indoors, a good way to avoid infected soil is to use one of the sterile soil substitutes discussed earlier. You can buy sterile soil or sterilize your own by baking it in the oven, though the latter is a smelly job.

About your only defense against buying infected seeds is to get them from a reputable dealer, or to get seedlings that are healthy. If you have any doubts about your seeds, you can kill diseases dormant on their surface by soaking them in a weak mixture of formaldehyde or some other similar-acting chemical. You can also dust them with zinc oxide, thiram, or copper oxide. Some seed diseases can be eliminated by soaking seeds in hot water.

Eventually, you will wind up spraying or dusting to rid your garden of infections. The methods are much the same as spraying for insects. Most of the traditional treatments for fungi are combinations of copper or sulfur. Recently, however, organic sprays have been developed that will do a good or better job, but they are usually quite specific in which fungi they will kill.

You should mix the fungicide with a spreading agent—wheat flour, powdered skim milk, soybean flour, mineral oil, casein, calcium, or caseinate—to make sure it sticks to the foliage and spreads all over it. Several commercial spreaders are on the market.

As with insect control, systemic controls have also been developed for many fungi. They are taken into the plants and prevent or minimize attacks.

Plants suffering from virus infection cannot be saved, and about the only spraying you can use against a virus is insecticide to limit its spread. Burn plants that you suspect are infected with virus immediately.

Before buying disease sprays, check with your county agent or nurseryman about insecticides and disease sprays that can be mixed together. Combining them will save you many sprayings. And if you suspect that your plants may be infected, cut off part of the affected area and get it to your county agent or state extension service for analysis. In that way you can have your problem identified and get a solid recommendation for an effective method of dealing with it.

Tables

Cold Hardy Plants for Early Spring Planting
Very Hardy
Plant 4-6 Weeks Before Last Frost

Broccoli	Onions	Spinach
Cabbage	Peas	Turnips
Lettuce	Potatoes	

Hardy
Plant 2-4 Weeks Before Last Frost

Beets	Chard	Parsnips
Carrots	Mustard	Radishes

Hardy
(Late Summer or Fall Planting)

Plant 6-8 Weeks Before First Freeze

Beets	Collards	Peas
Broccoli	Kale	Radishes
Cabbage	Kohlrabi	Spinach
Carrots	Lettuce	Turnips
Cauliflower	Mustard	

Cold Sensitive Plants
Plant on Frost-Free Date

Okra	Squash	Tomatoes
Snap Beans	Sweet Corn	

Plant a Week or More After Frost-Free Date

Cucumbers	Lima Beans	Sweet Potatoes
Eggplant	Peppers	

Summer Planting

Beans (All)	Sweet Corn	Squash
Chard	Soybeans	

Adapted from "Vegetables, fruits, and herbs: how to grow food cheaply" by Stoner, Brooks, and Williams, in *Landscape for Living: The Yearbook of Agriculture 1972* (Washington, D.C.: U.S. Department of Agriculture, 1972), p. 132.

Suggested Vegetables and Herbs for Greenhouses and Indoors

Bibb Lettuce	Swiss Chard
Mint	Thyme
Parsley	Tomatoes
Radishes	

Plants for Forcing

Witloof Chicory

French Endive

Rhubarb

Garden Trace Minerals

Element	Source
Sulfur	Organic matter, city water supplies, lime, some fertilizers, urban rain runoff, lime-sulfur fungicides, superphosphate, soil conditioners, gypsum
Calcium	Lime, some fertilizers, lime sulfur fungicides, soil conditioners, gypsum, superphosphate, organic matter
Iron	Specific sprays
Zinc	Specific sprays
Maganese	Specific sprays

Vegetable Insect Pests
(Harmful Insects)

Insect	Target Plants
Ant	Assists destructive aphids
Aphid	Globe artichokes, beans, broccoli, Brussels sprouts, cabbage, cauliflower, celeriac, celery, collards, cucumbers, kale, kholrabi, lettuce, mustard, peas, peppers, white potatoes, rutabagas, spinach, tomatoes, turnips
Asparagus beetle	Asparagus
Beet webworm	Beets, chard
Blister beetle	Beets, chard, white potatoes, tomatoes
Cabbage worm	Broccoli, Brussels sprouts, cabbage, cauliflower, collards, kale, kohlrabi, mustard, turnips
Celery leaf tier	Celeriac, celery
Corn borer	Corn, eggplant, peppers, tomatoes
Corn earworm	Asparagus, beans, corn, cucumbers, eggplant, okra, peppers, white potatoes, pumpkins, squash, tomatoes
Cutworm	Asparagus, beets, cabbage, broccoli, Brussels sprouts, cauliflower, chard, collards, kale, kohlrabi, lettuce, peas, peppers, spinach, tomatoes
Flea beetle	Beets, broccoli, Brussels sprouts, cabbage, cauliflower, chard, collards, eggplant, kale, kohlrabi, mustard, peppers, white potatoes, tomatoes, turnips
Garden centipede	Asparagus
Grasshopper	Practically any foliage
Grub	All roots

Pest	Plants affected
Harlequin bug	Broccoli, Brussels sprouts, cabbage, cauliflower, collards, kale, kohlrabi, mustard, turnips
Japanese beetle	Beans, corn, okra
Leaf hopper	Beans, carrots, celeriac, celery, eggplant, Jerusalem artichokes, lettuce, white potatoes, tomatoes
Lygus bug	Beans
Maggot	Beans, beets, broccoli, Brussels sprouts, cabbage, cauliflower, chard, collards, corn, kale, kohlrabi, mustard, onions, peas, white potatoes, radishes, rutabagas, scallions, shallots, turnips
Mexican bean beetle	Beans
Nematode	Cucumbers, okra, tomatoes
Pickleworm	Cucumbers, squash, pumpkins
Potato bug (Colorado)	Eggplant, white potatoes, tomatoes
Slug or snail	Lettuce, spinach
Sow bug	All seedlings
Spider mite/Red spider	Beans, celeriac, celery, corn, cucumbers, eggplant, onions, peas, scallions, shallots, tomatoes
Spotted cucumber beetle	Beans, cucumbers, pumpkins, squash
Squash bug	Cucumbers, pumpkins, squash
Squash vine borer	Pumpkins, squash
Stink bug	Beans, okra, tomatoes
Striped cucumber beetle	Cucumbers, pumpkins, squash
Thrips	Broccoli, Brussels sprouts, cabbage, cauliflower, collards, cucumbers, kale, kohlrabi, mustard, onions, pumpkins, scallions, shallots, squash, turnips
Tomato fruit worm	Same as Corn earworm
Tomato horn worm	Eggplant, peppers, white potatoes, tomatoes
Weevil	Beans, broccoli, Brussels sprouts, cabbage, carrots, cauliflower, collards, kale, kohlrabi, mustard, peas, peppers, sweet potatoes, turnips
Wireworm	Beans, beets, carrots, celeriac, celery, lettuce, mustard, onions, sweet potatoes, white potatoes, scallions, shallots turnips

Infection	Victim
Anthracnose	Beans, cucumbers, peppers
Ascochyta pod spot	Peas, peppers
Black leg/Black rot	Broccoli, Brussels sprouts, cabbage, kale, kohlrabi, sweet potatoes
Blights	Beans, celeriac, celery, cucumbers, peas, white potatoes, spinach, tomatoes
Club root	Broccoli, Brussels sprouts, cabbage, kale, kohlrabi, sweet potatoes
Damping-off	Almost any young plant
Downy mildew	Cucumbers
Drop	Lettuce
Dry rot	White potatoes
Fruit rot	Eggplant
Fusarium wilt	Peas, tomatoes
Leaf roll	White potatoes
Leaf spot	Beets, chard, cucumbers, peppers, tomatoes
Mosaic	Beans, cucumbers, lettuce, peppers, white potatoes, pumpkins, squash, tomatoes

Infection	Victim
Pink rot	Broccoli, Brussels sprouts, cabbage, cauliflower, celeriac, celery, collards, kale, kohlrabi, lettuce
Rhizoctonia	Broccoli, Brussels sprouts, cabbage, kale, kohlrabi, lettuce, white potatoes
Root rot	Peas
Rust	Asparagus, beans
Scab	Cucumbers, potatoes, pumpkins, summer squash
Seed decay	Beans, corn, lettuce, peas, spinach
Smut	Corn, onions, scallions, shallots
Tipburn	Lettuce
Verticillium wilt	Tomatoes
Wilt	Broccoli, Brussels sprouts, cabbage, cauliflower, collards, corn, cucumbers, eggplant, kale, kohlrabi, okra, sweet potatoes, white potatoes, pumpkins, squash
Yellows	Cabbage, carrots, cauliflower, celeriac, celery, collards, kale, kohlrabi, lettuce, spinach

Plant Disease Controls

Disease	Type	Controls
Anthracnose	Fungus	Do not touch wet plants; plant resistant varieties; rotate crops; copper fungicide
Asochyta pod spot	Fungus	Plant clean seeds/sets
Black leg-Black rot	Fungus	Keep garden clean; plant clean roots; rotate crops; eradicate wild mustard
Blights	Bacteria	Plant resistant varieties; rotate crops; burn affected plants; copper fungicide
Blossom-end rot	Physiological	Mulch; keep soil moist; lime; wood ash; calcium chloride spray
Club Root	Fungus	Sterilize soil; rotate crops; kill weeds; hydrated lime dust
Damping-off	Fungus	Fungicide dust on seeds before planting; sterilize seed
Drop	Fungus	Space plants; drain soil
Dry rot	Fungus	Plant resistant varieties; rotate crops
Fruit rot	Fungus	Plant resistant varieties
Fusarium wilt	Fungus	Plant resistant varieties
Leaf roll	Virus	Control aphids and ants; plant resistant varieties

Mosaic	Virus	Burn affected plants; control insects; plant resistant varieties; clear weeds
Powdery mildew	Fungus	Copper oleate; sulfur
Pink rot	Fungus	Rotate crops
Rhizoctonia	Fungus	Destroy affected plants; rotate crops
Root rot	Fungus	Drain ground; rotate crops
Rust	Fungus	Plant resistant varieties; sulfur dust; burn affected plants
Scab	Fungus	Plant resistant varieties; rotate crops
Seed decay	Fungus	Captan or other fungicide
Smut	Fungus	Rotate crops; pull affected plants
Spot	Bacteria	Rotate crops
Spot	Fungus	Clean garden plot; rotate crops; clear perennial weeds
Tipburn	Physiological	Plant resistant varieties
Tomato buckeye rot	Fungus	Mulch; captan; stake plants
Tomato leaf mold	Fungus	Plant resistant varieties
Verticillium wilt	Fungus	Plant resistant varieties
Wilt	Bacteria	Control insects; burn affected plants; plant resistant varieties
Wilt	Fungus	Burn diseased plants; fumigate soil; rotate crops; plant resistant varieties
Yellows	Fungus or Virus	Burn affected plants; control insects; plant resistant varieties

Insect Control Measures

Insect	Controls
Ant	Pour rotenone, pyrethrum and soap, boiling water into hills; chlordane
Aphid	Malathion; pyrethrum; rotenone; nicotine sulfate; lady bugs; strong water stream; soapy water spray; ryania; hand pick
Asparagus beetle	Rotenone; other beetle treatments
Beetle (General)	Hand pick; methoxychlor
Beet webworm	Pyrethrum
Borer	Prune infested areas; pick egg pods; rotenone; ryania; hand pick
Cabbage worm	Bacillus thuringiensis; rotenone; tar paper mulch; wood ash dust
Caterpillar	Methoxychlor; malathion; rotenone; sevin; hand pick; pyrethrum; ryania; salt water
Celery leaf tier	Hand pick; pyrethrum; ground tobacco dust; sulfur dust; rotenone
Colorado potato beetle	Hand pick; rotenone;
Corn earworm/Tomato fruit worm	Mineral oil; rotenone; ryania
Cutworm	Methoxychlor; shallow cultivation; hand pick; paper collar the plants; wood ash; mulch
Cucumber beetle	Methoxychlor; mulch; hand pick; screen cages over plants; rotenone; pyrethrum; interplant radishes; wood ash; hydrated lime spray
Earwig	Chlordane; sevin; mulch
Flea beetle	Rotenone; pyrethrum; wood ash-tobacco dust; carbaryl
Garden centipede	Hand pick; mulch
Grasshopper	Hand pick; rotenone
Grub	Cultivate to expose; malathion; sevin; milky disease spores; rotenone; ryania, hydrated lime dust; interplant garlic; trap crop

Insect	Controls
Harlequin bug	Hand pick; clear weeds; mulch; plant trap crop; sabadilla
Japanese beetle	Malathion; sevin; dig up grubs and expose; milky disease spores; rotenone; ryania; hydrated lime; interplant garlic; trap plants
Leaf hopper	Pyrethrum; rotenone; sulfur dust; malathion
Lygus bug	Pyrethrum; sabadilla; keep garden clean
Maggot	Pyrethrum
Mexican bean beetle	Hand pick; rotenone; pyrethrum; interplant marigolds; carbaryl
Nematode	Nematocides (Vapam, Mylone, or other temporary soil sterilizers); interplant marigolds; rotate crops; move the garden; clear weeds; green manure
Pea moth	Malathion
Pickleworm	Hand pick; rotenone; sabadilla
Red spider/Spider mite	Mineral oil; strong water stream; rotenone; sulfur dust
Snail, Slug	Metaldehyde; metaldehyde and arsenic mix; hand pick; mulch; hydrated lime; sand or ash mulch; carbaryl
Sow bug	Mulch; hydrated lime; hand pick; carbaryl
Squash bug	Hand pick; mulch; dust with wood ash-hydrated lime mix; sabadilla; ryania; carbaryl
Stink bug	Hand pick; clear weeds
Thrips	Rotenone; pyrethrum; nicotine sulfate; ryania
Tomato hornworm	Hand pick
Weevil	Hand pick; rotenone; resistant varieties

Vegetable Growth Data

Vegetable	Planting Season (approximate)	Time to Harvest (days)
Globe artichoke (perennial)	Spring	540
Asparagus (perennial)	Spring	365
Asparagus peas	Spring	90
Beans, green pod (bush)	Spring	45-65
Beans, green pod (pole)	Spring	56-72
Beans, lima	Spring	65-78
Beans, long pod fava	Spring	45-72
Beans, shell	Spring	90-100
Beets	Early Spring	55-80
Broccoli	Early Spring—Midsummer	70-150
Brussels sprouts	Fall-Spring	90-100
Cabbage	Fall-Spring	65-110
Cabbage, Chinese	Fall-Spring	70-80
Carrots	Early Spring to Fall	60-85
Cardoon (perennial)	Spring	110
Cauliflower	Spring-Late Summer	55-75
Celeriac	Early Spring-Winter	110-120
Celery	Early Spring-Winter	90-115
Celtuce	Early Spring	80
Chayote	Spring	90
Chicory	Early Spring	65-110
Chard, Swiss	Early Spring	55-80
Chives (perennial)	Early Spring	80
Collards	Spring-Fall	70-80
Corn, sweet	Late Spring	65-90
Cress	Early Spring	10-25
Cucumbers	Late Spring	55-75
Eggplant	Spring	70-85
Endive	Spring	85-98
Endive, Belgian	Fall	14-21
Garlic	Late Summer-Fall	100
Horseradish (perennial)	Spring-Fall	150

Vegetable Growth Data

Vegetable	Planting Season (approximate)	Time to Harvest (days)
Jerusalem artichoke (perennial)	Spring	150
Kale	Spring-Fall	55-70
Kohlrabi	Early Spring-Early Fall	55-62
Leek	Fall-Spring	60-130
Lettuce, head	Spring-Fall	45-76
Lettuce, leaf	Spring-Fall	45-50
Mustard	Early Spring-Fall	35-45
Okra	Spring	55-60
Onions	Spring-Fall	90-165
Parsnip	Early Spring-Late Summer	95-130
Peas	Spring-Fall	58-75
Peas, cow (black-eyed)	Early Spring	58-105
Pepper, sweet or bell	Early Summer	62-80
Potato, white	Spring-Winter-Year Round	90-120
Potato, sweet	Late Spring	120-150
Physalis	Spring	90
Poke (perennial)	Spring	20
Pumpkin	Spring	100-115
Radish	Spring-Summer-Fall	22-30
Rhubarb (perennial)	Early Spring	730
Rocambole (perennial)	Early Spring	100
Rutabaga	Spring-Fall	80-90
Salsify	Spring	120-150
Scallions	Spring-Fall	14-120
Shallots (perennial)	Fall	100-180
Soybean	Spring	90-150
Spinach	Spring-Summer	35-45
Squash, summer	Spring	50-60
Squash, winter	Summer	95-110
Tampala	Spring	60
Tomato	Spring	65-90
Turnip	Fall-Winter-Spring	42-55

Herb Planting/Harvesting

Herb	Type	Planting Season	Days to Harvest
Angelica	Biennial	Early Spring-Late Summer	70
Anise	Annual	Spring	75
Balm	Perennial	Spring	60
Basil	Annual	Spring	60
Bay	Perennial	Fall	80-110
Blackberry	Perennial	Spring	90-110
Borage	Annual	Spring	80
Burnet	Perennial	Spring	45
Camomile	Perennial	Spring	60-90
Caraway	Biennial	Early Spring	435
Catnip	Perennial	Summer	50
Chervil	Annual	Early Spring-Late Summer-Early Fall	75
Chives	Perennial	Spring-Summer-Fall	80-90
Comfrey	Perennial	Spring	30-60
Coriander	Annual	Early Spring	90
Cumin	Annual	Early Spring	90
Currant	Perennial	Winter	90-150
Dill	Annual	Spring	Foliage 70—Seeds 100

Florence Fennel	Annual or Perennial	Late Spring-Fall	90-120
Horehound	Perennial	Early Spring or Fall	45
Lavender	Perennial	Early Spring or Fall	90-120
Lovage	Perennial	Late Summer-Early Fall	40
Marjoram	Annual or Perennial	Spring	90-120
Mint	Perennial	Spring	30
Oregano	Perennial	Spring	45
Parsley	Biennial	Early Spring	70-90
Pennyroyal	Perennial	Spring	30-90
Rose Geranium	Perennial	Late Summer	60
Rosemary	Perennial	Spring	50
Rue	Perennial	Spring	45-60
Safflower	Annual	Spring	100
Sage	Perennial	Spring	75
Summer Savory	Annual	Early Spring	60
Sweet Cicely	Perennial	Late Summer-Fall	60
Sweet Fennel	Perennial	Spring	45
Tansy	Perennial	Spring	45-60
Tarragon	Perennial	Spring	60
Thyme	Perennial	Spring	50
Winter Savory	Perennial	Spring-Fall	45

Herb Use Chart

Herb	Root	Flower	Leaves	Seed	Whole Plant	Stem
Alexanders			●			
Angelica		●				●
Anise			●	●		●
*Balm			●			●
*Basil			●			●
Bergamot		●	●			
Borage		●	●			
Broom	●					
Burnet			●			
Caraway	●		●	●		
*Catnip			●			
Chamomile					●	
*Chervil	●		●			
Chives	●		●	●		
*Cicely	●		●	●		
*Coriander			●	●		●
*Cowslip		●				
Cumin				●		
*Dill			●	●	●	●
Fennel		●	●	●		●
Male Fern	●					
Finocchio/ Florence Fennel	●			●		●

Herb Use Chart

Herb	Root	Flower	Leaves	Seed	Stems
Foxglove			●		
Hellebore/Poke Root	●				
*Horehound		●	●		●
*Lovage	●		●	●	
Marjoram			●	●	●
Meadowsweet		●			
*Mint			●		
*Nasturtium		●	●	●	
Oregano			●		●
Parsley			●		●
*Peppermint			●		●
Rose Geranium		●	●		
*Rosemary		●	●		●
*Sage			●		
Sanicle			●		
Summer Savory			●		●
Tarragon			●		
Thyme			●		●
*Valerian	●				
Winter Savory			●		●
*Woodruff			●		●

*Plant has a distinctive aroma.

Mulch Substances

Peat moss	Sheet plastic	Spent mushroom compost
Sawdust	Ground corncobs	Hay
Rice hulls	Sugar cane	Pine needles
Wood chips	Ground or shredded bark	Grass clippings
Leaves	Spent hops	Straw
Heavy paper	Yucca fiber	Rotted manure

Insect Pest Controllers

Ant lions	Ground Beetles	Rove beetles
Aphid lions	Hornets	Syrphid flies
Assassin bugs	Lacewing flies	Trichogramma flies
Centipedes	Ladybird beetles	Wasps
Damsel bugs	Pirate bugs	Wolf spiders
Dragonflies	Praying mantises	Yellow jackets

Helpful Animals

Bats	Lizards	Snakes
Birds	Shrews	Toads
Cats	Skunks	

Editor: Jerome Fried
Art Direction: John Tullis
Illustration: Jack Lucey
Production: Sally Riggs
Typography: D & S Composing Service, Spartan Typographers
Lithography: Independent Printing Company